# Sex
## IS THE
# EASY PART

HOW TO *love* A
WOMAN FOR ALL OF HER LIFE

# JAMES CANTELON

Copyright © 2021 by Cantelon
Communications Group Inc.

All rights reserved. No part of this publication may be reproduced, stored in a retrieval system, or transmitted, in any form or by any means, except as may be expressly permitted by the 1976 Copyright Act or by the copyright holder in writing.

ISBN: 978-1-78324-234-4 (print)
ISBN: 978-1-78324-235-1 (ebook)

Whilst every effort has been made to ensure that the information contained within this book is correct at the time of going to press, the author and publisher can take no responsibility for the errors or omissions contained within.

Book design by Wordzworth
*www.wordzworth.com*

# **CONTENTS**

| | | |
|---|---|---|
| Introduction | | vii |
| Chapter 1 | Open Your Eyes | 1 |
| Chapter 2 | Gardening Ain't Easy | 39 |
| Chapter 3 | Be A Leader | 67 |
| Chapter 4 | Be Faithful | 83 |
| Chapter 5 | Lust, Adultery & Divorce | 99 |
| Chapter 6 | Be Friends | 107 |
| Chapter 7 | Our Love Story | 121 |

# INTRODUCTION

Anybody can do sex. But not everyone can do relationship. The tabloids trumpet lips, breasts, and butts – movie star A has it all, so does rock star B. They're a perfect physiological fit, their sex will be awesome. They marry. Three months later they split. What went wrong?

Great sex does not make a great marriage. In a relational vacuum sex suffers, and the law of diminishing returns kicks in. If the garden is neglected the fragile flowers soon wither. Only a strong relational commitment will see marriage succeed. Relationship, or the lack thereof, trumps chemistry every time. Sex can feed a relationship, but it never is the relationship. Indeed, without a man and woman committing themselves to one another, for life, sex becomes an orphan.

You often hear people say, "I'm in a relationship right now". What they often mean is, "I'm having sex". In our world sex *is* relationship. At the slightest hint of desire the clothes come off and the "relationship" begins. Pop culture thrives on superficiality – it makes perfect sense that relationships be superficial too. Sex becomes the common currency of social interaction. But its very commonness is inflationary. Just as one needs a wheelbarrow full of money to buy a loaf of bread in a failed state, so too one needs more and more partners and sexual novelty in the pursuit of love. Eventually the devalued dollar becomes worthless. And, ironically, the sexually "hip" sometimes become asexual. Disappointment, failure, and boredom in sex fuel a growing disenchantment with relational dislocation and dysfunction. Suddenly it's "cool" to be chaste, not out of moral conviction, but out of indifference. But, if there is hope (and there always is in the human breast), it is that one will be married happily with children. The latest "Holy Grail" of pop-culture is the "baby bump", children, home – some of Hollywood's biggest stars lead the cast of a new drama being acted out before the paparazzi of the world: "Family Values – the Return".

Unfortunately the swollen midriffs artfully portrayed on social media and in tabloids and Hollywood magazines have often given way to distraught, tear streaked faces as celebrity moms are gurneyed away to psychiatric hospitals, their small children under the care of inept boy-stars, themselves separated, self-absorbed, and alone. The "Holy Grail" has let them down. No one told them that children and home do not make a happy marriage. So what does? Are we all on some kind of downward slope to relational sorrow? Is joy in marriage an unachievable ideal? A lie? A black hole sucking all life away, leaving only a shell? Is that all there is?

Before going any further, I've got to make a confession: I believe in happy marriages because that's been my experience, both as a child growing up, and as a husband for over 52 years. In my formative years I was surrounded by

INTRODUCTION

parents, uncles, aunts, and grandparents who had forged strong, loving, sustainable marriages. All my models were positive. So, I expected my eventual marriage would be joyful, and that the marriages of my children one day would be too. Marriage failure was not an option.

But here's where my confession has to morph into a kind of disclaimer: my experience with marital dysfunction is all secondhand. I've been exposed to more than my share in counselling situations. But, after agonizing hours with distraught couples, I've always been able to go home to a totally loving atmosphere where peace and rest reside. So, as you read this book be aware that at times I may unknowingly, or unintentionally appear to be superficial in my comments, or at least naïve. Forgive me if anywhere it appears to you that I'm condescending, moralizing, or judgmental. Rather, understand that right from the first word I've committed myself to compassion, objectivity, and grace. I don't want to preach. I want to coach.

The book is written in seven chapters. Chapter 1 discusses the vital role of observation in the "startup" of a relationship. In the process several points are made with regard to understanding felt needs, and the impact of forgiveness. Chapter 2 is about "husbanding" or "gardening" a relationship. Here there will be a comprehensive overview of the care necessary for fruitful marriage. In Chapter 3 the absolutely most important truth about love is presented: love is not a function of how you feel, rather it's about decision-making. Sustainable, growing love requires "leadership decisions" that involve our intellect, emotion, and will. Chapter 4 addresses faithfulness. The point made is that faithfulness is more than sexual, it's also about commitment. This "C" word, as it's often called, seems to be the missing ingredient in so many marriages. In Chapter 5 a brief look at lust, adultery, and divorce, followed by Chapter 6, where the potential of marriage producing the deepest and most lasting of friendships is discussed. You won't want to miss Chapter 7 because it includes my wife Kathy's take on what I've written and some of her thoughts on what it's like to be a "loved" woman.

Once again, this book is not a final word, nor is it even an expert opinion. It is, however, a strong effort to address the breakdown of marriage with compassion and (I hope) wisdom. In a highly sexualized world we all need to know that when it comes to success in marriage, "sex is the easy part".

# ONE

# Open Your Eyes

It was red, sleek, and sexy. Sitting there by the curb it looked like it was moving at 100 mph. My heart pounded just looking at it. With the kind of reverence only a car-nut would understand I walked over. Just once in my life had I seen a Ferrari in the flesh. A work of art, a driver's dream, a boyhood fantasy, the ultimate – and here it was! I could reach out and touch it! I stood staring. Then I bent down to look inside.

In the bright sunlight it took a second or two for my eyes to focus on the darkened interior beyond the tinted windows. The shock was so sudden I actually gasped – the car had unsightly chrome bars and levers attached to the steering column. This living breathing legend had hand controls! This "redhead" was owned by a paraplegic, or an amputee. Suddenly the fantasy was eclipsed by the reality.

The Ferrari was a $250,000 wheelchair. I felt numb, and walked away chastened. I didn't even look back.

Later, upon reflection, I admired this paralytic for his or her élan, refusing to be inhibited, choosing to drive one of the fastest cars in the world. "I wish I'd met the owner," I said to a friend. What a great example of a positive attitude! But, I was thrown nonetheless by the vital life lesson I had learned: the outward appearance does not necessarily tell the story. You've got to get inside, beyond the fantasy to reality, a reality that may not only shatter the veneer, but even offend at times.

Susan and Dennis met at a birthday party for a mutual friend. They were both "single" in the out-to-impress, ready-to-compress their lives into a "meaningful relationship" mode (even though they both had been in and out of several failed relationships). The predictable happened: fateful introduction, overly enthusiastic response, "Oh! I've heard so much about you!!", offer to get her a drink, entry-level conversation, revelation of so many common interests, "No kidding! I love Tom Hanks!", casual physical touching, "meaningful" eye contact, and then, "How about dinner Friday?" Later, after the party, he thinks, "Wow! What a body!" She thinks, "He's so cute! And so nice! And so vulnerable! He shared his heart with me!"

Friday's date is hot. Sex afterwards is hot. He stays overnight with her. Saturday morning is awash in endorphins and romance. "This is the one!" they're both thinking. The next two months are a blur. Sex, and more sex. Talk of marriage (more enthusiasm from her than him), children, even time spent looking at condos. Then the weekend from hell.

> *They're hardly in the door and he's tearing her clothes off.*

It started out okay. Beautiful, slightly too expensive ("but who cares?") chalet in the mountains, gorgeous view, perfect. They're hardly in the door and he's tearing her clothes off. "Dennis! Not now. We just got here!"

"So?" he says petulantly, grabbing her belt. "I love you", the magic words to get his way.

"No!" she half shouts. "Not now! Besides I'm not sure you do love me".

"What?" An injured tone of disbelief. "What do you mean, I don't love you? We've made love hundreds of times!"

"Don't exaggerate. But that's the point. I don't think we've 'made love' at all. We have sex. But I don't think we have love."

"What the...!" Dennis unleashes a string of expletives. He rips the belt from her jeans and throws it at the patio door. Then he throws her on the bed and forcibly tries to take her. She fights him off. Bad to worse.

The next two days are full of revelation. He is demanding, angry, and violent. She is inward, teary, and bitter. He spends the whole weekend in his underwear, uses the toilet without closing the door, ignores her, and watches sports on television. She sulks and talks for hours on the phone with a girlfriend. But the kicker comes when she catches his reflection in the mirror through the open bathroom door as he anoints himself with some kind of cream from a tube in his shaving kit. She quickly puts two and two together.

"Herpes! You have herpes?!!"

"Nah. Not really. It comes and goes. It's no problem."

"No problem?!" She goes ballistic.

"You've given me herpes!" she yells with disbelief and rage. "You animal! You've given me herpes?!"

Dennis, embarrassed and angry, quickly dresses and announces, "I'm out of here. Find your own way home!" And he leaves without checking out. She is stuck with the bill, the herpes, and a broken heart.

Broken dreams might be more like it. How could this "nice, cute, vulnerable" guy turn into a monster? "How come I didn't see it?"

How come indeed? Wouldn't it be great if we could click a mouse and get a readout on the strengths and weaknesses of someone to whom we're attracted? A readout that goes beyond mere psychological testing, reading kind of like this:

## He

### Physical

- trim, 160 pounds, eventually will weigh 240 pounds
- good looks, will lose hair, develop potbelly

- athletic now, will become "couch potato"
- loves food, especially sweets
- given to flatulence, occasional drinking binges
- strong body odor, heavily masked by deodorant
- will develop adult onset type II diabetes
- tends to hypochondria, constantly complains about physical discomforts
- avoids physical labor
- ignores his nose and ear hair
- will have three heart attacks over the next 40 years

## Mental

- quick-witted, well read
- obsessive about "facts"
- likes to argue, and win
- will talk on and on about trivia
- low view of the arts
- defensive when his narrowness is challenged
- knows everything for sure

## Social

- terrific at smalltalk
- engaging, and even charming
- very status conscious
- sees a girlfriend as "trophy"
- sharp dresser
- loves to party
- happy to engage superficially

- manipulative
- ultimately a bore

## *Emotional/ Spiritual*

- no moral compass
- sees relationships as disposable
- given to depression
- afraid of commitment
- selfish, shallow
- feels more comfortable with "the guys"
- will spend more time golfing than husbanding when he marries
- a convivial follower, not a leader

## *Family Models*

- father was violent, beat his wife, left when the children were still in preschool
- mother caring, controlling, overprotective, given to depression
- both paternal and maternal grandparents divorced
- paternal grandmother alcoholic
- strong divisions between uncles and aunts
- family get-togethers rare, always end poorly
- no affirmation from family, only putdowns

## SHE

### *Physical*

- fit, petite, will weigh 110 pounds well into old age
- dislikes her appearance – will spend thousands of dollars on plastic surgery, diets, and breast augmentation
- has strong, two weeks per month, pre and post menstrual issues
- has one or two yeast infections per year
- is compulsive about makeup – will never allow her boyfriend and/or husband to see her without it, morning, noon, or night
- a picky eater, hates cooking, prefers eating out
- works out in the gym, three days a week
- will be osteoporotic
- fears aging, doesn't know she is sterile

### *Mental*

- very intelligent, straight A student
- strong in the arts
- reads the news everyday on internet
- buys books exclusively from the bestseller lists
- wanted to do a masters degree, couldn't afford it, wouldn't borrow, will live entire life regretting her lack of postgraduate education
- sees herself as a "liberal" thinker

## Social

- an extrovert
- presents well, always pleasant
- in a social setting tends to revert to a kind of protracted adolescence – life of the party
- overawed by success and the successful
- all her friends see her as "terrific"
- hates being alone

## Emotional/ Spiritual

- unhappy
- feels she's never been loved
- has no experience in emotional bonding
- will never achieve real intimacy, an emotional orphan
- finds it hard to believe whenever she's told by a boyfriend that he loves her
- conflicted about sex
- idealistic about relationship

## Family Models

- sexually abused by some of mother's live-in boyfriends
- intense argumentative interaction with mother, and siblings
- little, if any, joy

So, you click your mouse, and there you have it. But, chances are you'll ignore the information. Nobody's perfect, right? So true. He believes he'll save her, and make her happy – seems he's blinded by breasts. She believes he can make her happy, and she'll change him. The glossy picture of perfect bodies, teeth, and careless laughter promoted in the TV beer commercials, prevails. Total satisfaction awaits! The need to couple trumps everything else.

> *He believes he'll save her, and make her happy – seems he's blinded by breasts. She believes he can make her happy, and she'll change him.*

When I was 12 years old my father and I had a talk about love, sex, and marriage. This was one of several we had while I was growing up. This day he talked to me about choosing a girlfriend.

"So, Jim, the day will come when you'll want to have a girlfriend," he said.

"When, Dad?"

"Oh, maybe when you're 16 or 17." Little did he know that I'd been sweet on several girls since I was about nine!

"Let me give you a little advice. Before asking a girl out, watch her."

"Watch?"

"Yeah. You know. How she dresses. Who her friends are. What she laughs at. How she laughs."

"How she laughs?"

"What I mean is, does she giggle a lot? Is her laugh too

loud, a sort of attention getting device, brassy, hollow? She needs to laugh from her heart. It needs to spring from happiness."

"Huh?"

"You'll know what I mean when it happens. How does she treat people? Does she look you in the eye when she talks to you? Does she speak well of her parents? Does she show respect to the teachers at school? That kind of stuff. Oh, yeah, one more thing – try to meet her mother."

"How come?"

"Because her mom's her model. She'll be a lot like her when she's an adult. Then, try to imagine her mother married to me."

"Because I'm going to be like you, right?"

"Probably. This process will take you a month or two, but it'll be worth it. I call it 'due diligence.'"

I don't know how politically correct his comments were, but the same principle of observation could apply to either gender. Essentially he was saying, when it comes to choosing a mate, "Open your eyes."

Choosing a mate sounds old-fashioned. But that's what you're doing. You're not choosing a one night stand. You're choosing a companion, a friend, a lover, a partner, someone to whom you'll be joined at the hip. What's more, you're committing your life to this person. You better get it right.

So here is Mary, young, attractive, single, only a year into her job for a large insurance firm. She comes from a strong family, with great love from and for her mom and dad. She knows about the power of keen observation, and her eyes are wide open, because two "cute" guys have just joined the firm.

Dan swoops in to the office, a patina of sweat on his handsome face, a squash racket sticking out of a gym bag.

"Whew! What a game!", he says, a bit too loudly. "Beat you again," he laughs, "um, that would be 10 games straight, but who's counting? Ha! Tom talks a good game, but hey! I am the master! Ha! Ha!"

Tom, the vanquished victim, is the office manager. Red with effort, or embarrassment, he introduces Dan to the office, "Our new Communications Director. Known him since we were kids. I'm sure you'll all have met him before the day is done." Even as Tom walks to his corner office, Dan is introducing himself to everyone.

"Well, he sure is assertive," Mary thinks, somewhat blown away by this whirlwind of handsome self-confidence.

It doesn't take more than a few weeks for many to see that this whirlwind is destructive. Hard-driving and overly responsible at work (arriving an hour before and staying two hours later than anyone else), Dan, in a one- track, compulsive way runs roughshod over everyone. He's impatient, goal oriented, hard on the less successful, loud in his work ethic, and fiercely competitive. When things go wrong he shifts blame, is quick to criticize, ready to judge. Exaggeration and sarcasm continually pour from his mouth, and his humor is usually at the expense of others. But he's "cute", according to the women in the office, ready to flirt, ready to conquer the heart of some needy soul looking for relational fulfillment. But his eyes are restless and empty.

The other new guy, Ron, reminds Mary of her father. Diligent, but balanced, he quietly takes responsibility for his work, ready to learn. He doesn't need a lot of affirmation, but seems centered, self-directed. Flexible and tolerant, he asks non-directive questions of his workmates and brings out the best in them. He genuinely cares. Good-humored and easy-going, he exudes a healthy humility that makes him accessible and accepting. His eyes, alive and interested, betray no hidden agenda. In Mary's eyes, it's a no-brainer – "if I were to choose between them for a lifelong mate it would be Ron." Good choice. Her eyes are open.

As a potential spouse, she looks at Dan and sees conflict, conflict predicated on the stress of living with a self-centered, immature person who will never get over himself. She looks at Ron, and sees partnership, symmetry that comes from maturity, common interest, respect, good humor, and love. As it turns out neither guy becomes her husband, but she'll find the right person and for sure will marry "for life." It's not rocket science.

But it can be a crapshoot. No one's character and behavior can be scientifically predicted – we are free moral agents, after all. There may be a dark side in us that remains hidden, even to ourselves, until some unexpected stress comes along. What's more, there are gender differences which at times can place us poles apart. So, "open eyes" means awareness of the remarkable distance there is at times between how men and women view their world. "Closed eyes" means that you think the opposite sex thinks, and acts, like you do – the only difference is plumbing.

It starts in childhood, boys play war, girls play house. Boys compete, girls share secrets. Boys conquer, girls nurture. I know there are exceptions. And I know I'll be accused of stereotyping, but I'm only acknowledging something that the toy, video, and games industry lives by. Boys and girls have different interests. Appeal to those interests and you have a viable business. Understand those interests later in life and you have the potential for a successful marriage.

> *There may be a dark side in us that remains hidden, even to ourselves, until some unexpected stress comes along.*

Let's conduct a little test. Here are two people – Person "A" and Person "B". Who is the male, and who is the female?

## Person A

"Okay. So we've defined the goal. The question now is, "How do we get there"? First of all, we need to appoint a leader who will have command and control. He is to be obeyed by the rest of us – in descending order, mind you. We'll need a vice president, an executive director, several managers, all with authority over those beneath them. No decision will be honored except those made by the president and his executive committee who will not divulge information except on a need to know basis. The need for secrecy is because of the intense competition we face from our rivals. We've got to win. They've got to lose. No holds barred."

## Person B

"It's so good to be here together. How long has it been? We're here to make an important decision – but just as important is that we reach it together, agree, and leave this meeting as friends. Everyone's opinion matters, so we'll break into small groups to discuss each element of the decision in detail. Leave nothing out. Make no assumptions. I don't care how long it takes, I want the outcome to reflect our values, our experiences, and our feelings. We'll monitor the application of our decision over the course of the next several months. We want you to feel ownership, and to be empowered by the result. Everybody wins."

I know. There's a little bit of both in both. But who's the guy, and who's the gal? Your call.

Both of the monologues are given in a collegial context. So there's an element of civility and respect in the tone. But dig a little below the surface of the comments and what do you find?

"I'm looking for a fight " – "I'm looking for a friend"

"I want someone to lose" – "I want everyone to win"

"If you don't agree with me get out of the way" – "If we don't agree let's talk"

"Knowledge is power to help us win " – "Knowledge is wealth for all to share"

"We must obey the rules" – "We must affirm our values".

Obviously, if success is to be achieved, both A and B need each other. There are inherent weaknesses and strengths in each that will complement the other but there is also a great deal that potentially will cause each to say of the other, "I don't understand them. They don't get it."

So how do you create a "home " with these polarities in the foundation? Surely it will crumble. Unless.

A friend of mine was reflecting on his first year of marriage. Aggressive, combative, and intensely focused, he is married to his polar opposite. She is kind, flexible, and consensual in her approach to life, a potential doormat for his insensitivity. But she is also strong and relationally skilled. She doesn't shy away when he flares. She stands her ground. And remarkably the marriage is working well.

> *The culprit in a disintegrating relationship is indifference.*

"What I have discovered, Jimmy," he said, "is that I have to be sensitive to her needs. Hear her out, and respond with her perspective in mind." Sensitive to her needs. What a concept! There is genius in this concept. Why? Because conflicts begin with unmet expectations. And the culprit in a disintegrating relationship is indifference. Opening your eyes to his or her needs will cauterize selfishness and eviscerate indifference.

The place to start, if you need sensitivity training, is with the felt needs that are common to both sexes. Before we explore some of these needs let's consider an analogy. We often refer to baggage we carry, from our childhood, adolescence, our former relationships, etc. Usually the word has a negative connotation. Some baggage, however, can be positive. But the point is we all carry bags.

I fly a lot. Indeed, when asked where I live I'll sometimes reply, "Airplanes". At check-in I often marvel at the huge volume of bags people carry. So huge it looks like they're moving to another country and these are all their earthly goods. Others, carrying about as much, are only going on vacation but are prepared for every contingency. "You never know, it might snow in Florida this year. Did so back in 1938." Personally, I travel with a carry-on, nothing else. Even if I'm away for 4-6 weeks. I pack for three days, do my laundry in hotels, and spend no time in baggage carousels on arrival. No loss of luggage, no delays. But, I do carry a bag. We all do.

So, when it comes to "needs" the question is, "How many bags does he or she carry?" How many can he carry himself? Will she need me to carry her bags for the rest of my life? At what point will these bags be an encumbrance, not a pleasure? Do I want this?

Keep in mind that baggage usually is packed in order to sustain us on a journey. The downside is that it has to be carried. Without it, however, we don't last long. The trick is to carry only what you need. And, what a relief to put the bag away when its usefulness is done!

But then, some people become permanently attached to their bags. And as time goes by more luggage appears, adding clutter and bulk to an already encumbered life. The bags of course are invisible, but the stress of their weight shows in the eyes, alters the personality, and can even influence the character of the carrier. Eventually the spouse of this heavily laden laborer finds him or herself worn down too.

That permanent attachment, however, is often directly the result of love, duty, or obligation. For example: Barry met Anna at a singles bar. They were both there for the first time, both felt awkward, with great relief "found" each other and married. What they didn't find, until much later, was the baggage each was carrying. His was an overweening dominant mother who made life a punishment for Anna. Hers was a dissolute demanding 20-year-old son, who showed up at their door one winter's day, and wouldn't go away. The combined stress of these two pieces of luggage broke the marriage.

Okay. Enough about baggage. Let's take a look at the felt needs that are common to us all. We've got to start with these if we are are going to have a solid foundation for a sustainable relationship.

## A. "I just want to be happy"

Several years ago, on one of my TV shows, I interviewed a psychologist who at 75 years of age had remarried. He had been widowed two years after 50 years of marriage to his childhood sweetheart. Now, two years into his new marriage, he sat on the set an obviously happy man.

"Was it tough," I asked, "after 50 years of a happy marriage, to remarry? To start all over?"

"No. Not really. You see, I was very happy in my first marriage, so I assumed I'd be happy in my next. And I am. We are."

"How come?"

"Well, first of all, and most importantly, I married someone who was already happy. Someone who didn't need me in order to be happy."

"Huh?"

"A lot of people say I just need to find the right person to make me happy. I say, If you're not a happy single person, you won't be a happy married person. No one can make an unhappy person happy."

How true. Two things to keep in mind when entering a relationship: 1.You, regardless of your messianic complex, will not make her happy (you can, sadly, sour any residual happiness she has by unloving treatment). 2. No, you're not going to change her overnight. After the temporal "happiness" of infatuation, the romance of the wedding, and the sex of a honeymoon, you're both going to return to Ground Zero. You'll be more than physically naked. You'll be spiritually, mentally, emotionally, and morally naked as well. And, if you have nothing to give, if the whole exercise has been "to get", your marriage will soon be running on empty. The Irish dramatist, George Bernard Shaw, in Act I of "Candida" wrote (way back in 1898), "We have no more right to consume happiness without producing it than to consume wealth without producing it." The only way to make happy is to be happy, and give happy. And, if you try to survive by leeching another's happiness, soon you'll both be dried out.

> *If you try to survive by leeching another's happiness, soon you'll both be dried out.*

So what is happy? I'm going to go back to the Greek historian, Thucydides, who wrote around 455 to 400 BC. He said, "Happiness depends on being free, and freedom depends on being courageous." The English poet Coleridge (1796 to 1849) wrote that freedom is "a universal license to be good." These wise men are onto something. Freedom is only free when the liberated person limits himself to doing good. If freedom means un-limits then one abuses, steals, bullies, demands, and forces one's way, regardless of the cost to oneself or others. On the other hand, there is genius in dealing from a position of strength and courageously serving someone else, meeting their needs, loving them. Happiness is a byproduct of seeking the other's good. Or, to put it another way, happiness is fuelled by loving.

## B. "I want to be healthy"

Of course. Who would want to be sick? We all want to be healthy. What's more, in our universally narcissistic culture, we want to be "buff". Because buff means desirable, as one 40-something guy sweating and grunting away at the bench press beside me in the YMCA gym said to no one in particular, "I do this for sex. Women want fit guys." For sure – mentally fit, morally fit, emotionally fit, relationally fit. Healthy is a lot more than "six- pack" abs of steel. Healthy means "made for the long-term". Healthy means "holistically, comprehensively balanced." A healthy person is the "gift that keeps on giving" to a marriage – the spirit is continually being renewed, therefore giving is never exhausted. Like the amazing human heart that keeps on beating, a healthy person keeps on running. For a lifetime.

And where does this loving begin? By listening. No kidding. One of the most profound contributors to health is the knowledge that someone cares enough to listen to us. Someone who allows us to be their focus. Indeed, this leads to our next felt need.

## C. "I want to be included"

This could also be stated, "I want to be valued," or, "I want to be respected." The most painful sense of this need occurs early on when the kids in the park are choosing sides for a game of baseball, basketball, or some other team sport. As each choice is made, you feel increasingly devalued. The worst is to be chosen last. Have you ever taken stock of how much of your time, treasure, and talent is expended on acceptance? We want to be cool – so, cool clothes, cool car, cool looks, cool kids, and cool costs. We want to be outstanding, but we don't want to stand out. The ultimate horror is to be the wallflower at the prom. Ours is a three-step dance: include me, value me, respect me. And we never tire.

I think I was about eight years old when dad, in one of our sex/relationship talks said, "When you're married tell your wife you love her 12 times a day."

"Whoa! That's a lot! Don't you think once is enough?"

"No."

"Why?"

"Because a woman can never be told enough that she's loved. When you tell her you love her she feels accepted, respected, and valued. What's more, her contentment and happiness will come back to you."

"How's that?"

"Well, she'll be the center of a happy home. Every guy wants, and needs a happy home. In fact, as they say, your home will be your castle when your wife knows she's loved."

I took his words seriously because I saw him every day practicing what he preached. Hugging my mom. Coming up to her and kissing her neck. Playfully slapping her backside. Telling her she was beautiful. Telling her he loved her. Time and time again, every day, every year. What can women do when so affirmed? Flourish. And shine.

## D. "I need to be understood"

To understand someone is to see them as they are, to imagine them as they were, and as they will be. Like David understands Mary.

It's their third date, a black tie affair at Mary's company's Christmas party. He looks sartorial, she looks stunning. Three times at the party David whispers to her, "You are beautiful!" Three times she blanches and says, her voice terse and almost frightened, "No! Don't say that!" He's amazed at her fervor. He's even a bit hurt. But he understands.

His best friend's sister is a good friend of Mary. In fact she set them up. Before he asked Mary out he had a good long talk with this sister. He found out that Mary had been raised in a very unhappy home where she was both physically and verbally abused. She was always put down, never affirmed. She was told she would never be beautiful, never amount to anything. And, being told this again and again, year after year, being called a "slut" by her mother every time she was sexually abused by one of her mother's live-ins, she became totally convinced she was ugly, unlovable, and worth nothing. Fortunately she went to a good high school where a guidance counsellor infused in her a sense of intellectual integrity, and gave her a work ethic that saw her graduating with a scholarship to University. There she excelled academically, and became a lawyer. Now she's working for a large corporation, master of her work, and still victim of her upbringing. That's why she just can't handle it when David calls her beautiful. She would be much more able to cope with putdown. But, he is gently persistent, sensitive, caring, and patient. And she's just now beginning to believe that maybe she is beautiful. It'll take several years of loving cultivation to bring her to the point of accepting her beauty. But she will. Why? Because David understands. He'll love her, marry her, affirm her, and patiently bring her to that point. He understands.

### E. "I want to be trusted"

If anything is at the core of sustainable love, trust is it. Trust is solid, unshakable, secure. It provides the footings for the foundation of a strong relationship. Jealousy, on the other hand, provides sand as a foundation – shifting, eroding, unsettled, insecure. Insecure people are jealous people. Secure people trust, and are trusted. And, interestingly, when we're trusted we tend to act in a trustworthy manner.

When we trust someone we rely on their character. We believe in them, in their honesty, truthfulness, sense of right and wrong, and their honor. We are confident in their word – they do what they say they'll do, and follow through on their promises and commitments – there is no hidden agenda.

Mind you, even the most trustworthy person has no hope of a sustainable relationship if they happen to engage with someone who at the core is distrustful of everyone. The distrustful person is a controller. Take Allison for example.

It started when she was six years old. Her father, whom she loved totally, left her and her mother. At first her mom tried to tell her he would be back. But in her heart Allison knew that would never happen. She had a huge sense of betrayal and a broken heart. Deep, deep down, something triggered within. She would protect herself from ever being hurt again. No one would get her unqualified trust. She would see the world through a self-protective lens. From now on everyone would have a secret agenda but she would not be sucked in. She would out-think, out-maneuver, and out- manipulate anyone who tried to get close. Yes, she had needs. Yes, she wanted to be loved. She would play the game to see those needs met, but she would never give her all. She would be in charge.

And she was. So much so that every guy she attracted eventually caught on to the fact that Allison was an overbearing, jealous dictator who flew into fits of rage, or descended into tears and whining to get her way. Dating her meant bondage to constant "where were you, who was that I saw you with, what are you going to be doing on that fishing trip, are you sure no women are going along"? Constant suspicion. Constant innuendo.

She did find someone to marry, however. He's a simpering little fellow who hangs on her and needs to be told what to do. She despises him. Almost as much as she despises herself. Distrust has destroyed her capacity to truly love and be loved.

> *Distrust is toxic. Trust, on the other hand is life-giving, and life-affirming.*

Distrust is toxic. Trust, on the other hand is life-giving, and life-affirming. Craig is a case in point.

He was orphaned at three and spent the next five years of his life bouncing from foster home to foster home. Rootless, and alone, he became inward and distrustful because every time he gave his heart to a new "parent" they would move him on to a "foreign" home. Emotionally his cupboards were bare. He failed Grade 1.

Then at age 9 he was adopted. He was enveloped in a tsunami of love. In fact, he nearly drowned. It was like a hurricane of culture shock. He wanted to escape and hide under a bed, like a new pet cat had done in one of his former homes. He was dislocated and afraid. He didn't understand the language of love.

His new parents understood. Very gently they folded him into their lives. Patient and forgiving, they gave him no reason to reject or rebel. Their trump card was trust. He was thrown by it. They let him do things. If he wanted to stay in his room they let him. If he wanted to go for a walk, or shoot baskets at the local playground, they let him. If he wanted to just disappear for a few hours, they let him. No questions. No suspicion. No cross examination when he got home. They trusted him. It was almost intoxicating. And, to his wonder, he found himself wanting to live up to their trust. Slowly but surely trust rebuilt his life and gave him a future. Today he's a successful businessman with a happy home, a very content wife, and four loved children. And his adoptive parents are dearly loved grandparents, like a solid rock, foundational to his family's life. Trust begets trust.

Not only do we all want to be trusted, we need to be trusted. It's like food to the soul.

## F. "I need to be inspired"

Inspiration is the polar opposite of boredom. Inspiration produces enthusiasm which in turn fuels inspiration. Boredom produces indifference which in its turn fuels boredom, or to put it another way, if you want your relationship to thrive you've got to be inspired by it. You need to show enthusiasm, act enthusiastically. If on the other hand you're indifferent, the relationship will die. Boredom is a killer.

I remember as a teenager reading about the breakup of a famous Hollywood marriage. He was every 14-year-old's hero, handsome, athletic, able to "leap buildings in a single bound". She was gorgeous. Young girls tried to dress like her, young men dreamed of marrying her. But they broke up. Why? As a young person I just didn't get it. Wasn't physical chemistry enough? Then I read about their life in an exposé written by an investigative journalist who had been given exclusive interviews with them both. Bottom line, they were "married singles", both self-absorbed and insular. His idea of living was television, golf, and clubbing with his male friends. Hers was shopping and sleeping in. Neither lived for anything bigger than themselves. Neither cared for anything or anyone but themselves. They were both empty suits. With empty heads and empty souls. Little wonder neither was inspired – their marriage was like a Ferrari without an engine, a beach without a horizon, a lyric without a song. As the American poet John Berryman wrote, "my mother taught me as a boy that to confess you're bored means you have no inner resources." If you're not inspired you sleepwalk.

So what inspires us? A dream. Noble behavior. Great need. Great art. A far horizon. Heroic action. You name it. Generally we're inspired by something bigger than ourselves. Something that breaks us free from self. Something that pulls the best out of us. And, if you'll let it, there's no greater entry-level "inspirer" than marriage.

How's this for inspiration? "I'll love you every moment of your life from this day forward. I'll cherish, nourish, and care for you in sickness or in health. We'll climb every mountain, and cross every valley together. We'll be joined at the hip. We'll have children together, they'll become the finest, most well-adjusted, loving adults they can be. We'll take adventures together and when death does us part we'll care for each other to the dying breath. When we die, we'll die like we lived: content." Faithfulness. Fun. Focus. Fervency. Fruitfulness. Forever. Alliterative bliss!

## G. "I need significance"

This could also be stated, "I need to be challenged", or "I need to do something meaningful", or "I want to leave a legacy". Deep down we all know we're here on planet earth for a very brief time, "a poor player, who struts and frets his hour upon the stage, and then is heard no more," as Shakespeare put it. We want to leave the world a little better than when we entered it. We want to leave a mark.

Over the years as a TV interviewer I have met some very successful, wealthy, and famous people. One of the privileges of the art is time spent before and after the show with a guest in the "Green Room". Often it's there, without the TV cameras watching, that the truth comes out.

The Actor: "You know, Jim, I'm very well known but I'm not known well, if you know what I mean."

"Go on," I say.

"Well, my face is on the buses, and the billboards, in fact my name is everywhere, but no one really knows me outside my famous self. For instance, no one but my few good friends know I'm diabetic, I'm afraid of heights, my number one love is, was, and always will be my high school sweetheart who was killed in a football accident. They don't know that I hate my work, that I feel insignificant as someone who merely entertains people, that I need medication to sleep at night."

"Why the insomnia?"

"It's not that. It's a feeling of uselessness. I mean, all I do as an actor is mouth someone else's words and pretend to live some fictional character's life. And for this people love me and pay me. I want to do more than this."

The Politician: "It's all a charade you know."

"What is?"

"Those televised government sessions on CSPAN. I mean, we know the cameras are on. We're acting. Posturing. It's all phony, the bluster, the outrage, the self-righteous burst of indignation. Off camera we're friends."

"You don't have differences?"

"Of course we do. But, for most of us politics is a job – a fairly cushy one too. We're happy to leave it behind on the weekends when we can. Very few of us truly want to serve the public."

"Really?"

"Yeah. Really. Why else the fighting over cabinet posts? Staff. A private car. More money. Prestige. It's about ego."

"Sounds cynical."

"Because it is. Guess I've been in it too long. Can't wait to get out of it and do something useful."

The Author: Clank. Clank. Clank. Labored breathing. I hear someone walking with obvious difficulty down the hall to the Green Room. A heavy figure appears, leans against the doorjamb, face running with sweat, his crippled legs braced with heavy steel.

"Are you Jim?"

"Yes. Come in."

"Whew! What a morning! I just came from the network morning show. What a joke."

"What do you mean?"

"They gave me five minutes to recap the entire history of the Irish Republican Army, then they cut to a weather man in a hot tub! Can you believe it?"

Yes I can. Too many producers, directors, and interviewers should have a clear message tattooed on their foreheads,

"As if I care". Little wonder they too are cynical, and in their reflective moments wonder what they're doing with their lives. Fame is theirs, but significance eludes them. Many fight self disgust.

Unless we're total dolts, sooner or later we're going to take stock of our lives. The major questions will be, "What have I done with my life? Have I made a difference? If I had it to do over again, what would I change? Does anybody care that I'm here?"

> *Unless we're total dolts, sooner or later we're going to take stock of our lives.*

Significance. Without it our hearts sour.

## H. "I need to love and be loved"

This need is huge! Indeed, the remainder of this book is essentially about how to love.

But, a few general comments first. We've all seen entertainers flushed with the crowd's adulation blowing kisses at the thousands of adoring fans saying, "I love you! I love you all!" Well, we know that's not only not true, but also impossible. What they're saying is, "I love your applause! Give me more!" Even though we say we "love the world" or "love all of Spielberg's movies", as if in one sweeping statement we can embrace everyone and everything, the truth is that love demands focus and exclusivity. The young man in the heat of hormonal fire may dream of having sex with every girl he meets but, even though he has the potential, as C.

S. Lewis put it, to "populate a small village", in his heart of hearts what he really wants, and needs, is "one true love".

An old ballad says, *"The wind doth blow today, my love,*
*And a few small drops of rain;*
*I never had but one true love;*
*In the cold grave she was lain.*
*I'll do as much for my true love*
*As any young man may;*
*I'll sit and mourn all at her grave as*
*For a twelvemonth and a day."*

UNKNOWN

The picture of a young man huddled in the cold grey rain at his true love's graveside is both bleak and romantic. Even though it appears a bit melodramatic it captures a truth: our very deepest longing is to love and be loved by one special person.

What's more, this exclusive love is forever – faithful, true, unwavering, "till death do us part". It's ironic that in a world where about half of our marriages end in divorce this "forever" love is still the subject of most modern ballads, and the holy grail of romantic novels and television soap operas. And, if we were to look at our western world's fascination with lasting love with the eyes of some alien observer, we'd note the great gap between the ideal and the real. For most of us love doesn't seem to last, but our intuitive nature wants, indeed needs it to last. We long for sustainable love. We will never give up, it seems, on dreaming about one true love at our side till our dying breath. In an unfaithful world, we desperately need faithfulness.

Faithful love creates a clean environment in which the soul thrives. When you love and are loved you live in a context where patience and kindness, consistency and trust, temperance and hope, growth and maturity prevail. You and your loved one are low maintenance: that is, no jealousy, no ego trips, no fits of pique, no rudeness or abuse. You're seldom if ever, "off-putting". You live for the other. And the other lives for you. True love covers "a multitude of baggage". And, it doesn't take a genius to figure out that a great lover is not always a great "liver". Someone who truly loves you will live true. And we all know, the truth sets us free.

There certainly are more felt needs than I've so briefly described, but the wonder is that we are often blind to them, at least as they relate to the other person. We are navel gazers, unable or unwilling to see the broad horizon awaiting those who rise above their preoccupation with self. We just won't grow up.

But what if you want to grow up? You just don't know how. Obviously, it has nothing to do with the number of candles on your birthday cake. We all know people in their 70's and 80's who are very self-centered and immature. Where do we cross the divide between "it's all about me" to "I'm only a small player"? Where do we lift our eyes from the nine square yards we occupy to the vast horizon? Where does maturity begin?

I think it begins the very moment you are able, for the first time, to forgive. At that moment you truly, as if for the first time, open your eyes. In Jane Austen's "Pride and Prejudice", the main characters, Miss Elizabeth Bennett and Mr. Darcy, are just getting to know one another when, in a conversation Darcy says this:

> *"I have faults enough, but they are not, I hope, of understanding. My temper I dare not vouch for – it is I believe too little yielding – certainly too little for the convenience of the world. I cannot forget the follies and vices of others so soon as I ought, nor their offences against myself. My feelings are not puffed about with every attempt to move them. My temper would perhaps be called resentful. My good opinion once lost is lost forever." (Chapter 11)*

When Darcy confesses his "temper" is "too little yielding", he sounds contrite. But he's not. In fact he is proud of his resentful nature – it speaks well of his discernment and judgment, so he thinks, to say that his "good opinion once lost is lost forever". Why? Because it flatters his conscience. Conscience is unyielding and sometimes too radical in its insistence on what is right and wrong. We refer to it as our "moral compass". Without regard for how "magnetic north" was established early in our lives, we proclaim self-righteously that conscience is our guide, oblivious to the legalisms, the hurts, the half-truths, distortions, and the sub-cultural values that blended into the intuitive sense of right and wrong with which we are born. Ultimately, conscience is the lens through which we see and interpret the actions of others. As such it can provide focus or distortion, clarity or confusion. But it will not yield to perceived injustices where it has been assaulted by the actions of others. It sees itself as right and the other as wrong. There is no middle ground. It cannot see anything or anyone but itself. That's why forgiveness is so difficult. Conscience has an innate desire to be right and needs always to see the unrighteousness of the other person's actions. Forgiveness appears "weak", an endorsement of bad behavior.

> *Forgiveness is foreign to our nature. And, as with all foreignness, we tend to fear and reject it. It's counterintuitive to put ourselves in the other guy's shoes.*

To judge and condemn is a natural reflex when we've been injured by someone. Even if we've had no prior exposure to the law there's something deeply ingrained in our nature that passes judgments cannily reflecting decisions of the court. It seems and feels right to seek and perform justice. Unlike the court, however, our judgments are not blind. Self-interest clouds our vision. Forgiveness is foreign to our nature. And, as with all foreignness, we tend to fear and reject it. It's counterintuitive to put ourselves in the other guy's shoes.

So, in that our inwardness is prejudiced against forgiveness, we've got our work cut out for us if we are to achieve the objectivity necessary to show grace. It has to come from outside ourselves, and that's one of the great benefits of maturity. An adult can see the big picture. A grown-up has eyes. Open eyes.

And only the adult can be merciful. Whereas our conscience-fuelled calls for justice seek to burn bridges, forgiveness seeks to show mercy. Which is why forgiveness is so powerful. Rather than forever shut away the offender, forgiveness provides a pathway to reconciliation. In the realm of human relationships mercy trumps justice every time.

So, "How often does one forgive?", someone asks. "What if my husband is unfaithful and abusive? I confront him. Threaten to leave him. He weeps, says he'll never do it again. All is well for a month or so, and it starts all over again. At what point do I say 'Enough!'?"

Only you know when enough is enough. But know this: forgiveness is not an enabler of dysfunction. If forgiveness becomes codependency it has ceased to be forgiveness. To forgive does not mean to forget.

One can show mercy without forever binding oneself to an abusive spouse. If your husband has broken the marriage vows by abuse or unfaithfulness, the agreement is broken – you are under no moral obligation to tie yourself to his selfish behavior. Forgive and move out. Show mercy and move on. There's no requirement that you be reconciled as mates. But, forgiveness keeps the bridge open, so you may be reconciled as human beings somewhere in the future. You'll not be married to him, but you'll at least be able to look him in the eye and treat him with courtesy and civility. "We're not speaking!" is the language of children.

Victoria, 38 years of age, married for 17 years, with three sons aged eight, ten, and twelve was blindsided by the news. Her husband had just asked for a divorce. She had no warning. She had no suspicions. She couldn't believe it. It was surreal.

Those international business trips the past three years? All accompanied by a female executive assistant who had become his lover. On top of that, several short-lived affairs over the years. Blow on blow. He's in love. The executive assistant has his heart. He wants out. Wants to stay "friends". Original stuff.

He leaves that day. Doesn't tell his sons. She's shell shocked. Cries herself to sleep, anxiety like she's never known. Her life is over. "What am I going to tell the boys?"

A scenario like this occurs a few times every day in North America. Devastating and dislocating as it is, the discarded wife and confused children somehow survive and make it through. The kids grow up, fall in love, get married, and the father, now separated from his third wife, ghosts around the fringes of his children's wedding pictures. He wants back in, but there's no room. Life has moved on.

Good thing then, that Victoria had a friend who gave her wise counsel. "Time. Give it time. I know you want to castrate him! But remember, the story is not over. Your sons love him, and their future choices are in the balance. If you diminish him in their eyes they'll be diminished too. They need to think as well of him as possible. Bitterness on your part will only hurt you. Better to forgive and move on. Take the high road."

Victoria took that friend's advice. Today, 30 years later, her sons are happily married, she has six grandchildren and holds no bitterness. Her ex is the loser. He marginalized himself, incrementally fading from his sons' view with every new "love". Now he's tolerated, but inconsequential, forgiven, but irrelevant. He blew it. Victoria, on the other hand, lives with dignity and meaning. Forgiveness empowers her to rise above her circumstances and do the right thing. She's a grown-up.

Simply put, opening your eyes means being objective. It means clearing your lens of the detritus accompanying unchecked infatuation. It means stepping back and taking a long, hard look. After all it's your life you're dealing with here. It's your history, your story. You want it to be a great story.

## TWO

# Gardening Ain't Easy

When I was a young boy I lived with my parents in a small town in Saskatchewan. It had a population of about 600 and was a lonely stop for the steam locomotive that used to come chugging to the solitary grain elevator every week or so during the harvest season to pick up wheat. The town had one main street, a grocery store, a dry goods store, a drug store (a real luxury), and a humble little church. Dad was the pastor.

We were very poor, but my brother and I didn't know it. Our ignorance of our material lack was, perhaps, due to the joy in our home, and the downright fun we had running free in the tiny hamlet. For us it was a "Tom Sawyer" kind of life. It surely was a more stressful life for Mom and Dad, but they very rarely, if ever, showed it. They were rich in internal resources. And, they were young. Both in their twenties, they overflowed with the "optimism of youth" and seemed undaunted by "the slings and arrows of outrageous fortune" as Shakespeare put it. They may never have heard of the latin expression, "carpe diem", but they certainly knew how to carp the diem. Terrific. They were terrific.

This doesn't mean they were alike.

Mom was the more delicate of the two. First of all, she was very beautiful. Whenever I've looked at some of the pictures taken of her in those years I've seen why Dad was attracted to her. She had been born and raised in Northern Ontario to a family that had its share of troubles due to my grandfather's alcoholism and womanizing. He was self-educated, a robust, hard-working, outgoing guy who had been raised without much of a moral compass. He embraced life. Unfortunately for my grandmother, he embraced more than he should.

So, as the middle child of three sisters Mom was caught not only in occasional sibling issues, but also in the intense dramas that often accompanied her father's episodic drunken excesses. More than once her mother would escape the home in the night, her three little girls in tow. As time went on Mom chose to sleep in the basement. There she had a sense of her own space and some measure of control.

Her home life like that of many other dysfunctional homes wasn't all bad. Her parents did love each other, and her father could be not only charming but loving. Later in life, morally and spiritually reformed, he was a wonderful man.

I knew him in those years and have only warm memories. He loved us, and we loved him. But there's no doubt Mom grew up with an instinct for survival. Her backbone was strong.

Dad, of course, was less delicate (twice Mom's size), and certainly less complex. Not that his upbringing didn't have its challenges. First of all, his mother was taller than his father. Secondly, they were what the British say, "like chalk and cheese". Grandpa was outgoing, Grandma was inward. He was short and tough, she was tall and elegant. He was hilariously social, she was asocial. Dad says they loved each other, at least most of the time. But there were moments when the best thing for the four kids to do was hide behind the couch and wait it out.

Interestingly, Dad was a hybrid. Tall like his mom, strong like his dad. Reserved like his mom, but socially skilled at the same time. Visionary like his dad, but tempered in his enthusiasm for the journey like his mom. And when it came to living it was embrace not retreat. Nothing seemed to bother him. He had no need to control. He was just as happy to careen. This ability to function when out of control was a real asset in the rough-hewn prairies of that time. Life was unpredictable and hard. There are so many stories... I'll tell you some of those stories as the book goes along. But for now let's get back to the garden.

I mentioned we were poor. So poor, in fact, that we lacked what development people these days call "food security". To help us along, one day my visionary father announced, "Shirl, I'm going to plant a garden". Whereupon he immediately went next door to our neighbor's to borrow a spade. The humble parsonage was located on a large double-wide lot, most of which was rock-hard, quack-grassy, non-arable soil. It had a penchant for growing tough, persistent dandelions and thistles, and seemed bent on defeating Dad as he tried to break the surface with the spade. Any experienced gardener would have at least used a pickaxe, but such luxuries were unknown to us. In fact, over the course of my upbringing I don't recall Dad ever having the right tools for the job. He made do, whether it was plumbing or electrical challenges, with a hammer, an axe, and yards of duct tape. As it happened, within ten minutes of full-bodied stabbing at the impenetrable soil, the spade handle broke. Dad spent the next two hours fashioning a rough-hewn handle from a stray hardwood branch, with his axe. Unflappable, and uncomplaining, he carried on. "Much better handle", he muttered, as Mom looked on in dismay.

His shirt soaked, his eyes stinging, and his nose dripping with sweat, he persisted for two days, until a small fallow lot was ready for planting. As a five-year-old I rejoiced at the outcome and declared with excitement, "Wow Dad! You've done it! You've got a garden!"

"Not yet son," he said. "Now I've got to plant something. And not just anything. It's got to be something that will grow here. And then I'll have to cultivate, water, and weed it, before we get a crop". I was somewhat shaken. I didn't know a garden needed so much care.

To my everlasting delight Dad said I could have some space to plant my own garden. Immediately I started planning. I decided I'd plant carrots. I loved eating carrots right out of the earth, dirt and all. It crunched and ground in your mouth with an explosion of flavor. I could just imagine the delight as I crunched away on my own carrots, picking the dirt from my teeth. That very day Mom and I walked to Fraser's General Store and bought several small paper packets of desiccated seeds. "Here, this one's yours," Mom said, handing me a magic packet of carrot seeds. I still remember the rattling sound as I shook it. I felt like Jack and the Beanstalk. It was all I could do to not break out into running home. But I walked at Mom's pace, my heart bursting with anticipation. Tomorrow I'll have carrots!

A few minutes later I carefully dug little holes in a row and planted the seeds in my corner of the garden plot. I tamped the soil down and assiduously watered each spot. I imagined each seed springing to life. I hardly slept that night.

I rushed out at dawn and was crushed to find not the slightest sign of life in my row of carrots. Nor was there any evidence of growth in the other rows of vegetables Dad had planted. Downcast I slouched back into the house. Dad was in the kitchen. "Dad," I complained, "nothin's growing." He patted me on the head, "Don't worry, son, give it time. You'll have carrots soon". But I wanted to know how soon. "Ohh, about two to three weeks, maybe, I'm not sure." What?!

I couldn't bear it. Surely something was happening. I went out and dug up one of the seeds. Nothing. I replanted it and sat in the dirt. This was going to be painful. Waiting was no fun. No one had warned me that gardening required more than water, fertilizer, and cultivation. Patience was vital. Vision and patience. Who knew? I managed to hold off for a week. Then it happened! I woke up to a few slender, frail shoots of green breaking through the soil. Excitedly I pulled one up. I was shocked to find nothing but a skinny little white thing dangling at the end of the squiggly green thing. I bit it. Tasted like grass. I was not pleased.

Over the course of the next ten days or so I managed to ravage at least half of my "crop". When the carrots were pencil-thin I'd had it with patience. I pulled them all up, and that night we had "baby carrots" for supper. The really big, fat, dirt-covered carrots didn't appear for another two weeks. They were from Dad's rows, but I loved the crunch, and the dirt. As I wiped the carrot mud from my lips I knew I'd learned something. I just wasn't sure what. Dad used a big phrase, something about "delayed gratification".

Most of us want immediate results. Whether it's a garden, an education, or a relationship, we find it hard to let something develop at its own speed. This is why so many singles opt for one-night stands. The need for instant gratification (impatience) trumps all else. The one-nighter, of course, never satisfies. There are no shortcuts to satisfaction. It requires maturity to let love grow. Like a garden...

## Choosing the Soil

These days it's not cool to say you're looking for a wife. Since the sexual revolution of the mid-twentieth century the operative word is "relationship", which is far less demanding than "wife". Relationship implies shelf-life, a "best-before-date", a convenient opt-out option, whereas wife means commitment. Wife means life. Precious few guys are prepared to go that far. And women have come to expect that men are basically noncommittal, to the point that they too aren't prepared to go that far, although, in their "heart of hearts" wish they could. In this regard women are, in my wife Kathy's tongue-in-cheek words, "morally superior". Argue all you will, but when it comes to the patterns of history, it seems that women have generally preferred nest over chest.

Ok. So you're looking for a relationship. Where do you start? The internet? Singles bar? A "lonely hearts club"? To work the analogy you've got to find a place to plant a garden. You've got to choose the soil. And what will you choose? Arable or non-arable? Weedy or verdant? Stony or malleable? Lots of either-or's here. Occasionally it can be both-and, but seldom. The guts of it is, you've got to choose.

Love, like life, is built on choices. Indeed, I firmly believe we don't "fall in love", we "decide" to love. Let's face it, the very notion of falling suggests accident, randomness, injury, short-term incident, powerlessness, distractedness, blind fate, coincidence, unintended consequences, confusion, to name just a few. But it's amazing how powerful that moment of being blind-sided is. In the overwhelming

> *Love, like life, is built on choices. Indeed, I firmly believe we don't "fall in love", we "decide" to love.*

passion of that experience we're willing to jump out of the airplane without a parachute, hang-glide without the glider, leap without looking. It seems we're wired for self-destruction. This, of course, can be very ennobling. We'll "climb the highest mountain, swim the deepest sea, ford a piranha-infested river" for our new-found love. Our inner hero comes to the fore. For a moment we're profoundly selfless. And selflessness is always good. For one thing it makes us very attractive. For another, it's the very zenith of the human spirit. A great heart is a selfless heart. Little wonder the girl is swept off her feet.

But the fall is very quickly followed by choices. They begin as seemingly inconsequential, increasing in magnitude as the relationship progresses (or regresses). Which night? Friday or Saturday? Which restaurant? Which movie? Whose party? Your place or mine? Your parents for Christmas or mine? And they keep growing in complexity until "yours or mine" morphs into a fledgling "our". Then again, it may never reach that point. For many, a tug-of-war escalates between "mine and thine", until the inevitable split ends the conflict, and the combatants go off to lick their wounds and find someone else to test their immaturity.

Sounds grim. Mainly because it is. Life-decisions always have their grim side because there are consequences, good and bad, pleasant and unpleasant. Pretty much every choice we make impacts at least one other person, sometimes several, and can reverberate for years. The choice right now? Who are you looking for?

Before I launch into this any further, let me make a disclaimer: Not one of us is perfect, and for every concern we may have about a possible mate we can be sure that she has just as many about us. I'm not a utopian. The ideal will always escape us, but there can be real beauty and satisfaction in two imperfect people bonding through the power and discipline of sustainable love.

So who ARE you looking for? A "mother for your children" (I personally find this one gag-reflex inducing)? A "sex-kitten"? A "soul-mate"? A "kindred spirit"? A "friend"? All of the above? And, does it matter to you where she's been nurtured? Is it of any concern to you whether she had/has a loving father, or, for that matter, a father at all? What kind of mother would be optimum? If she was raised by relatives, or was moved around from foster home to foster home, does that bear any notice? Do you want a happy person, or someone who will make you happy? You should be able to tell by the second date whether she's high or low maintenance. Does it matter? (I once counselled a newly married guy who was fatigued with his new wife's needs. I said to him, "You married an 'exotic', a 'Ferrari' of a girl, who is fun but high maintenance. You're going to have to do a lot of maintenance."). Who are her friends? What are they like? How does she spend her time? Does she laugh from her heart, or does she giggle? Is she self-confident, or insecure? How many boyfriends has she had? Is she thoughtful? Is she "eager"? Maybe too eager?

I could go on, but here's the point: All of these questions, and many more, give insight into the "soil" of her soul. They help you appreciate the nutritional ingredients that have produced this currently beguiling female. They tell you what to expect if you continue to see her. They give you fair warning. But then, in the intoxicating grip of infatuation, who wants to be warned?

## Preparing the Soil

If you're of the female persuasion you may be a bit put off by these gardening headings. Don't be. They're just literary tools (metaphor, simile, analogy) to help us guys understand how important it is to truly "husband" someone as valuable as you. We can be klutzes. We need help. I'm trying to give a little. Read on.

When Dad started working on that impossible vacant lot he broke the handle of the spade, and nearly broke his back in the process. But he knew that this initial effort was absolutely foundational to success. He could have done what farmers in the ancient middle-east used to do (as some still do today) and "broadcast" the seed by throwing the seed out over the untilled ground (before ploughing!), hoping that some would take root, even while most would be eaten by birds, destroyed by the sun, or trampled on by animals and humans. He chose, however, to do what history has taught the good gardener. He "worked" the soil. He dug and turned the soil over, painful shovelful by shovelful, broke up the rock-hard clumps, clump by clump, until the plot was what may have been termed "fallow" soil prepared for planting.

The way to work the soil of a new relationship (as well as a mature relationship) is by affirmation. "What?" you exclaim. "Affirmation? I thought you said 'work'." I did. Affirmation takes and is work. Without work affirmation is mere flattery. To truly affirm a girl you've got to be observant and thoughtful. For example, Henry drives to Jackie's house to pick her up for their second date. She's in third year university and still lives with her parents. He remembers the first time he dropped by her dad was out in the front yard mowing the grass. This time her dad's not in the yard, but the grass is freshly mowed and the shrubs newly trimmed. Jackie comes to the door looking awesome, obviously having prepared carefully for the date. Henry looks at her admiringly and says, " Hey Jackie, you look terrific!" As she responds with a demur "Thank you", Henry continues, "and so does the yard. Your dad is quite the gardener." "Yes he is," she says happily, "he takes care of everything with a lot of pride." And Henry, with a warm smile, says, "Obviously. Takes good care of his daughter too, no doubt." She glows, "You've got that right. He's great! Super guy." And the date gets off on the best note possible. Why? Because Henry in a few thoughtful sentences affirmed Jackie, her father, and her relationship with her dad. He made her feel good about herself, accepted, and admired. He showed respect.

Affirm, affirm, affirm. And affirm again. No man can show enough, no woman can receive enough. The first ingredient in sustainable love is affirmation. If you're going to live a long life of long love you've got to be passionate about building her up, holding her in high esteem, recognizing the inner princess that every girl secretly wishes to be. She needs to know that she's the centre of your universe, and the sovereign of your heart. So in every way, and everyday, show and tell her that she is. Never quit.

Remember that the mortal enemy of a strong relationship is not another woman, but indifference. Think of loving a woman as a call to duty. The one thing a soldier cannot do is lose focus. When on duty one's self is eclipsed by the need for vigilance and selfless action. A distracted sentry often ends up court-marshalled. Keen focus and unrelenting faithfulness to duty wins the day. Similarly, you've got to be on guard against taking your girl for granted, assuming that her needs are being met, that she's happy just because she has you. She needs to know that YOU have HER. That you cherish her. That you honor and respect her. And never forget that attraction is easy, but distraction is easier. The sentry who sleeps is the loser.

> *Remember that the mortal enemy of a strong relationship is not another woman, but indifference.*

Affirmation, however, is more than verbal. Trust, for example, is non-verbal affirmation. When a woman is trusted by her guy she feels valued. It means that even though she's "his", she's also her own. She is not under his control. Indifference isolates, but control stifles. Control betrays trust. In fact it strangles it. No woman, unless she's terribly insecure or emotionally damaged, can "breathe" when there's an equally insecure man managing her every move. If you're going to succeed in this relationship she's got to be free – free to make her own decisions, free to include/

exclude you in the process, and free from cross-examination. This freedom affirms and builds her up. It makes her a co-equal in a cooperative enterprise. You're not just partners, you're friends. Affirmation is the language of friendship. So much so that the future garden will not survive without it.

## Choosing the Seed

It's a simple question here: What do you want this garden to produce? In the gardener's parlance, is it to be a vegetable garden? A flower garden? An "English country garden"? A sunny garden or a shade garden? A private or a "show" garden? What's it to be? Your choice. Choose the seed and choose the future – you "reap what you sow". So it goes without saying if it's your life and hers that are in the balance you want to choose wisely.

To put it another way, what are the priorities that in your heart MUST be in place in order to have the kind of long-term love that you desire? Undoubtedly they'll include some or all of the following: happiness, fun, health, sex, kids (?), affluence, friends, growth, holidays, home, faith (?), peace, and whatever else may come to mind. These are not only priorities, but expectations. Analyze them carefully, because another mortal enemy of long-term bliss is the erosive drip-drip-drip of unmet expectations.

I'm not saying that expectations are cast in stone. Indeed, a healthy stock-taking can free you of, or modify, some of your longest held expectations. But the point is we have them, in most instances unspoken, yet powerful in their hold. For example: Tom and Alice had a very intense dating life and married six months after their first date. The subject of children had come up a few times, but neither of them expressed their true thoughts because neither wanted to risk disagreement. A year into the marriage Alice asked Tom to go to a fertility clinic with her to see why they had not conceived as yet. Tom didn't want to go. The truth was that he was quite happy to be childless. She was stunned at this revelation and asked the obvious question, "Why didn't you tell me you didn't want children?" Tom responded with, "Why didn't you tell me you DID?"

Years ago I was driving somewhere and listening to a radio phone-in show about gardening. The expert guest (whose name escapes me) was truly enthusiastic about his skill. He referred to gardening as the ultimate human achievement, and then said something I'll never forget: "Gardeners harness the sun." Whoa! How profound is that? And so true.

You can't garden without light. The critical player in all plant life is photosynthesis – "putting together with light". This is the process (as we all remember from our high-school science classes) whereby the chlorophyll in the leaves of plants absorbs light energy produced by the sun, combines it with water and minerals from the earth and carbon dioxide from the air, creating food that is stored in the stems or roots of the plant. Without light there is no photosynthesis. Without photosynthesis there is no plant life. Without plant life there is no animal life. Hide the sun and it's a downward spiral. Light is vital to a sustainable world.

So too, love is vital to a sustainable marriage. "Phileosynthesis", to coin a term, "putting together with love", needs to be understood if the gardener (the husband) wants to harness the energy that true love produces. He will need knowledge, skill, and faithfulness.

> *Beauty and peace require both an engaged mind and a bent back.*

To husband means to "till, cultivate". The old English word "husbandman" refers to a farmer. Husbandry is farming or careful management. The husband/farmer/gardener needs to balance the growth requirements of his plant material with yield (if farming a crop) or design (if gardening) elements that will produce the intended result. A farmer wants food. A gardener may want food as well, or he may simply want the lines, colors and textures that produce beauty and peace. But make no mistake. A garden doesn't just happen. It is designed, planned, and cultivated. Thought and sweat. Brain and brawn. Beauty and peace require both an engaged mind and a bent back.

## Climate Zone – Is She Cold or Hot?

Apparently there are ten climate regions in the Northern States and Canada, graded from 1 to 10, coldest to hottest. What grows in Zone 10 will die in Zone 1. For example, palm trees can thrive in Southern Ontario along the shores of Lake Erie (at least for the summer if transplanted), but they have no chance in Northern Ontario where winter temperatures can sometimes dive to 25-40 degrees below zero! A magnificent Douglas Fir loves temperate, wet, coastal areas of Washington State, but shrivels and dies in the semi-arid regions of north-central Idaho. In order to grow, plants must find the "sweet-spot" between the minimum and maximum temperatures of the zone. The amounts of rainfall are critical – not too much, not too little, just right. Wind speed (prevailing?) is a factor as well. As are the length of the frost-free period and the depth of snow cover in the higher altitudes or latitudes. It takes a delicate balance to produce the most slender sapling or the mightiest oak. The nature of the plant demands it.

So, husband-to-be (or husband already), you've got a gardening challenge. Here are some key questions you must both ask and answer:

## What Does She Like?

This sounds simple enough. But it's not. We all shrink from rejection, so when we're asked what we like we tend to respond with what we think the questioner wants to hear. We're so eager to make it work we gloss over our true feelings and create a fantasy world with our conversation.

First dates can be a remarkable exercise in superficiality.

She: "Oh! I'm so glad you enjoy the theater! I absolutely love it too!" (She's been twice, but sees it as "cool".)

He: "Oh yeah, I go all the time." (He went to see "The Sound of Music" twenty years ago with his Grade 4 class.)

She: "I love the dancing, the music, the colorful costumes."

He: "And the sound system."

She: "Absolutely! There's no audio like live theater."

He: "I did sound when I was in school."

She: "Really! Wow!"

He: "Yup. Organized it all for a Grade 8 production of "Tom Sawyer" (three mics and two speakers.)

She: "Oh. Wow!" (Who is Tom Sawyer?)

He: "Y'know, 'Tom Sawyer' isn't exactly live theater material (said with a knowing look of authority), but our teacher wrote the music, adapted the story, and then taught the actors how to act. It was great!" (It was a total disaster.)

She: "Oh yeah. Tom Sawyer's one of my favorite stories." (Who *is* Tom Sawyer?)

And on, and on... little wonder with this kind of exuberant phoniness at the root the "relationship" doesn't last. It's like a seed that falls on thin soil. It may sprout, but the lack of depth of soil sees it dried and fried in no time by the sun and the wind.

It takes time and keen observation to find out what she likes. Again, the initial flush of excitement trumps likes and dislikes. But, as time goes on she'll reveal her hand.

For example: my wife Kathy and I met as teenagers at a summer camp. One evening, on our first walk together, I tried to take her hand. She very quickly pulled it away. We continued walking but I was more than a bit surprised at her reluctance to hold hands. Then to my amazement about two hundred yards further she took it. I was flummoxed. What gives? It took several more walks to discover that she was shy of any public displays of affection, and would take my hand only when no one was around. At this point in her life and development this was what she liked. Her comfort zone existed within an envelope of privacy. Today she likes to kiss in public! Go figure.

But that's the point. Likes and dislikes come, go, and change as maturity increases. What you liked at sixteen you may dislike at twenty-four. But, to engage your life with someone else's you've got to be like and dislike aware. Likes and dislikes are sort of like the cogs in the wheel of a mechanical watch – engage them proactively and intentionally and the watch keeps excellent time. Miss or damage a cog and the watch stops until repaired.

Don't shake your ahead and grimace with your guy friends when talking about your girlfriend, "Man! All she wants to do is talk! I mean, she _loves_ details! Drives me crazy!" If she likes to talk, if she likes details, talk and give her all the details. That's what she likes. That's who she is. Are you dating boobs and a butt, or a person? She may also like long walks, hot drinks on cool evenings, watching romantic comedies, spending time with her girl-friends, ice-cream, being alone at times, whatever. It's up to you to observe what she likes and comply. You are responsible to know the "min and max temperatures" of her growth zone. Sometimes your likes and hers will clash. Either compromise or give in. Fighting over likes is immature.

All she needs to know is that she's the center of your universe. Your garden craves attention, focus, and unfailing love.

> *All she needs to know is that she's the center of your universe.*

Give her that and she thrives. What's more, your unrelenting care will come back to you. A woman who is given all will give her all. Your garden will nourish you, and will be a place of beauty and peace.

Everyday tell her you love her. Every day <u>show</u> her you love her. Include her in your life, even in its smallest decisions. For instance, you're walking to the corner store to get some milk. It's a ten minute walk. Ask her if she wants to join you. It's a rare woman indeed who can resist a walk. Walking with her husband is an opportunity for unbridled, uninterrupted attention. Even if you just walk without talk. You've thought of her. You've included her. This is the language of love for her. The rain is falling. She blooms.

Take note of all that she does both in and out of the home. Show appreciation. Mention specifically what it is you're grateful for. "Boy! You're a terrific Mom. I loved the way you comforted Sally last night. You always have the right thing to say." Or, "What a great daughter you are! I mean, you drive to their home every week, two hours in the car, and give them such care. I'll bet your mom loved those gorgeous flowers you brought her yesterday." You can't give this praise if you haven't been a keen observer. Nor can you "pull it off" in an insincere way. You've got to mean it. Affirm. Affirm. Affirm. She's in your care.

## What are the Constant Stresses in Her Life?

These are the "prevailing winds" that constantly buffet her, making life a 24/7 "bending before the wind".

Ellen is a terrific person. Married three years to Peter, she has proven to be loving and low-maintenance. Maybe too much so. Keen to comply. Ready to compromise. Doing backflips to avoid confrontation. Hiding something.

Hiding what? It will be another five years before she confides in Peter. And she'll do it only because she knows he truly loves her. Her life at home as a young girl was a horror of almost nightly sexual abuse by her father. Every time she sees a middle-aged man she remembers. Every time she and Peter have sex she remembers. Every time she sees a young girl she remembers. Every day she leans into the prevailing winds of dark memory.

This is why she resisted Peter's compliments in the first few years of their relationship. She truly didn't believe that she was beautiful, talented, or special. Over time she learned that he meant it. She learned how to mask her feelings of unworthiness and self-contempt. But the reflex still betrayed itself non-verbally, creating a gap in their intimacy.

Because of her love for Peter, a man who has proven his love for her, she manages a tendency to neglect her appearance, not caring how she dresses. It's deep within her, this desire to be as unattractive as possible to all men, but deeper still is the root of worth that has dug into her soul, worth that is "new every morning" because of Peter's husbanding. Slowly her "climate zone" is changing. Only faithful husbanding over many more years will finally overcome those prevailing stresses. Peter's love will eventually become a stand of trees protecting her from the erosion those winds create. Lucky Ellen! Lucky Peter.

There are, of course, any number of other prevailing winds that people live with. Physical, emotional scars. Mental challenges. Poverty. Bereavement. Dysfunctions. Depression. You name it. But if you as a husband are going to bring the best out of your wife, you've got to know the "climate zone" in which she was born, raised, and presently "grows". Otherwise you'll misread her, misunderstand her, and your relationship will wither.

## How Much of the Year is She "Under Snow"?

As I write these words I hear Tony Bennett's voice on our home sound system singing, "I love the winter weather where my love and I can get together... I got my love to keep me warm." Winter can be very romantic. Very cozy. Very beguiling, especially at Christmas. But it can also be very harsh, bitingly cold, and intimidating. I think we all have a great love for it, and great respect. Now Tony's singing "Walking in a Winter Wonderland". Right now I love it. Winter can be very life-affirming. Plant life in the northern climates often depends on the snow to insulate life while lying dormant beneath it, but it can also be life-threatening. Cold can chill the bones and cut off the flow of blood to the extremities. It can kill.

I hesitate to get into snow and winter in the life of relationship, because it's such a subjective area, an area where most of us, when challenged, get defensive. But the fact is that none of us are monotone in our state of mind or feelings. Sometimes we're moody. Sometimes we're gloomy. And sometimes we just need to be alone, or be left alone. Space. We need some space.

The key is to know when to leave her alone or, to have the wisdom to leave her "mood" unchallenged. Whenever someone gives us a "cold shoulder" whether outside of marriage or in it, we tend to take it personally. Maturity enables us not to. She's chilly today. That's ok. That's cool. I'll help her incubate by not meddling or demanding much of her right now. She'll thaw.

> *The key is to know when to leave her alone or, to have the wisdom to leave her "mood" unchallenged.*

The reasons for the cold can be almost anything – depression, time of month, conflict with or lack of friends, money issues, insecurities, illness. You name it. A wise gardener recognizes and allows for this season. He doesn't demand that the flower bloom all year round.

### Where is the Light and Where is the Dark in her Life?

Even the most inept gardener understands one thing: some plants thrive in constant sunlight, others in shade. Some require both a bit of sun and a bit of shade. Others bloom in the morning, some in the evening. And some bloom only for a day. The goal is to find the steady state where the plant's full potential can be realized.

So, does your wife need constant sunshine? Constant shade? Or a little of both? Don't say you don't know. You've got to know. If you don't, find out. Keen observation will do it. Is she an extrovert? Does she need the sunshine of social interaction? If so, make sure she gets it. Or, does she prefer the shade, loving to be by herself, doing artistic things, reading, thinking? If so, give her alone time. And if her needs don't exactly jibe with yours, so what? Your goal is to be the best gardener possible. A successful husband knows what's required to produce the best bloom. He doesn't take it personally if his wife needs special care, because he realizes that marriage is not about him, but about her.

Maybe her sunshine is her kids, grandkids, or weekend adventures. Whatever it is give it to her. Don't resent the effort. It pays. Remember, her joy comes back to you in spades. Maybe her shade is long walks with you, going to the theater, quiet evenings with one or two longtime friends. Again, meet those needs. She'll flourish, and so will you.

Remember, sunshine lightens her eyes. You'll see the sparkle and hear the buoyancy in her voice. Shade strengthens her spirit. You'll sense the stability and peace in her heart. Shade deepens her.

And yes, shade can lead to night. Sometimes her life is dark. The darkness may be rooted in things like unresolved childhood issues, former broken relationships, or a lifetime of disappointment. Whatever it is, if you know what it is you're already more than half-way to helping her heal.

But, when all is black, don't take it personally. Deal from a position of compassionate strength and be her anchor.

## What Waters and Feeds Her Soul?

I haven't heard too much lately about talking to plants. When I was a teenager it was the big fad, all kinds of hippie-type gardeners extolling the virtues of gentle conversation with the trees, flowers, and vegetables in their lives. Sounded air-headed then. Still does.

But – and this is a big "but" – there certainly is a case for conversing with your spouse. For your wife, especially, it waters and feeds her soul. The challenge for most men, however, is the "how to?" How do you talk to a woman? What interests her? What does she want to hear? What does she want to say? It's so intimidating!

Not necessarily. Forget about the "how to". Focus on two things: 1. Ask questions.

"Questions? What questions?" Easy answer: any questions about her feelings will get you started on a long conversational path. Feelings about herself – "How does that (whatever it may be) make you feel?" About her friends – "Man! That comment of Alice's must be upsetting for you!" About her kids – "You looked pretty proud when Johnny recited that poem in front of the whole school." About your marriage (prepare for a looong path here!) – "So, it's been eight years. How are you feeling about our marriage? What's good? What's bad? How do you feel we should change?" Feelings fella! She wants to talk about feelings!

2. Listen. Then listen actively. Look her in the eye. Nod and respond. Keep your mind in gear. Which means focused follow-up questions in direct response to something she's just said. Restate what you think you've heard. Ask if that's what she meant. Register with her that you get it. "Oh yeah. I hear you. Sure. Of course. I understand. Go on…" Just as a garden needs regular soakings of water to be healthy, your wife needs regular conversations (long and deep) to flourish.

*Feelings fella! She wants to talk about feelings!*

Expert gardeners tell us that watering relieves plant stress. Drought, cold, harsh winds, and other environmental phenomena do stress the flowers, trees, veggies, and other delicate life in your garden. Watering comforts and preempts crisis. So too does good conversation in your home.

Another gem from the world of gardening wisdom is that a well-watered garden apparently will have a strong immune system re: most pests and disease. You don't have to do much damage control (via pesticides) with plants that are properly hydrated. It's amazing how a consistent regimen of conversation in marriage will fend off dysfunction. It highlights bad habits or behavior, provides consensual remedies, and encourages accountability. It refreshes the soul of your relationship.

We're also told by gardening gurus that watering releases nutrients to a plant's roots. I don't know the science of this but what a concept! Imagine, your conversation with your spouse can release nutrients to your family root system. It feeds your bond. It makes you strong.

## What's in Her Closet?

Storage is critical to good gardening. You need storage bins, storage sheds, and sometimes storage yards (depending on the scope of your garden). Storage is comprehensive: you store tools, seed, heavy equipment, odds and sods, stuff you'll use, and stuff you'll never use again but are too attached to or too lazy to get rid of, out of sight out of mind. Most storage is useful, some storage is septic. Sooner or later you have to do a spring cleaning, get the good stuff in order, and get rid of the bad stuff. Which is rather like what we do with our closets.

"Closet", of course, has come to mean much than the place where we store our clothes. It's now the thing some people "come out of" and it's also the place where many store their baggage. It has become the dark repository of secrets, bad behavior, and memories. And, in terms of your wife's overall makeup, the closet is also her "roots" cellar.

I was astonished to discover in my reading that plants breathe through their roots as well as their leaves. This is why we aerate our lawns and gardens. If the earth is too compacted the roots are starved of life-giving oxygen. So, you've got to "open the closet door" and let the fresh air in.

When you open that door, be very careful to be compassionate and non-judgmental as she reveals the bad stuff. She's showing great courage and trust by revealing the dark things. She is taking you into her confidence, truly giving you her heart. Respect her for it. And deal tenderly.

> *Tenderness is the holy grail for women.*

Speaking of tender, there is an old love song entitled, "Try a little Tenderness". Tenderness is the holy grail for women. They can't resist it. Why? Because you can't fake it. It's from the heart, not the head. It shows profound consideration, and total regard for the other. It places one in the other's shoes. It is the eyes of love, food for the soul, water in a barren land.

## THREE

# **Be A Leader**

For most of us fast-food can be irresistible. Whether the saltiness or the sweetness tempts us, it's so satisfying to dig into those potato chips and chocolates. Our taste buds soar and we want more. If we lack restraint the whole bag or box can be gone in minutes. The lead-shot weight in the stomach and/or the heartburn follows, and we reach for the antacid...

Falling in love can be a bit like fast food. The sugar-high of infatuation gets the heart pumping and the hormones racing. Even though the chips and chocolate may eventually sour the soul, the initial free-fall is exhilarating. The grass is greener, the sky bluer, and all is gloriously well.

Falling has no meaning, however, if there is no landing. At some point one's feet have to meet the ground. And the landing can be rough. Lack of control may be heady, but one's head must be in gear when on terra firma.

Perhaps this is why Susan is broken-hearted. Tina Turner's hit song, "What's love got to do with it?" is her current lament. Three months ago, when she fell in love with Dennis, her heart was awash in excitement, anticipation and dreams-come-true. Now it's bitter tears and regret. What went wrong?

Wholesale surrender, as in a premature (immature?) plunge into blind, unbridled wish fulfillment, the beguiling embrace of a fantasy, that's what went wrong, for both of them. She saw love and marriage. He saw sex and more sex. If romancing her led to the bedroom, and if sleeping with him led to long-term relationship, then both were on a compelling adventure. It was the stuff of movies.

Movie plots, of course, have little to do or say about the business of living. Love and life are inextricably joined at the hip in the ongoing stress of day-to-day responsibilities and contingencies. The discipline of intentionality is a basic requirement of existence in the real world. Sustainability demands it. And the key to sustainability is the engagement of three very necessary components: intellect, emotion, and will. Let's start where most of us start: emotion.

Sometimes people say they "fell in love at first sight". It's as though a spontaneous chemical reaction occurred the moment they saw each other. That visceral reaction saw their knees buckling, their hearts fluttering, their eyes dilating in a helpless moment of total attraction. One stricken guy put it, "I felt like an electric current was flowing through my body." In a flush he knew that "she was the one."

Most of us need that revelatory emotional kick to get moving. None of us tend to love what we don't like (though we'll see that it *is* possible to do the loving thing for unlikeable people). We resist any pressure to engage emotionally unless we're smitten. But once the bug has bitten we're on a mission. Coordinates are exchanged and the texting, emails, and phone calls begin. We find it hard to sleep at first. The intoxication of infatuation has thrown us completely off-balance.

There is more to it than infatuation, however. There's this thing called desire, a natural human longing for a number of good things like food, rest, home, the beautiful, the admirable, and sex. Desire contributes greatly to a full life. Yet, if not tempered by wisdom and self-control it can reduce life to a treadmill. Indeed, out-of-control desire can destroy even desire itself. The Rolling Stones classic hit, "I can't get no satisfaction", is a sober hymn to dissipation. Covetousness and greed are proven slippery steps on the downward slope from healthy desire to cankerous obsession. Addiction, whether it be to material wealth, power, or sex, is the dark side of desire.

Novels and movies would lose much if not all of their intrigue if this dark side did not exist. Readers and viewers demand sex and violence. The passions and consequences of plots depicting unbridled hunger for status, money, power and sexual conquest boil with emotion. The magnetic draw of the vicarious and the voyeuristic is hard to resist.

We're told, however, that there are some personality disorders that render a person devoid of feelings of love, hate, regret, joy, or whatever. I'm not qualified to comment other than to say that most of us do not suffer this anomaly. We feel. And we feel intensely. Sometimes even the smallest stimulus can see us soaring the heights or drowning, as Bunyan put it, in "the slough of despond". The waters run deep.

> *We can fall out of love as quickly as we fell into it.*

Ironically those deep waters of emotion often run shallow. We can fall out of love as quickly as we fell into it. There are shoals beneath the surface, the most treacherous being immaturity, the most subtle being novelty.

One does not have to be a psychologist to recognize the chief characteristic of immaturity: selfishness. It's all about me. The distressing thing about self-absorption is that it can prevail throughout an entire lifetime. There's many an eighty-year-old out there who still thinks the world revolves around him/her. Little wonder their relationships with spouse, children, extended family, neighbors, and workmates have been fraught. Their navel-gazing and aggressive or passive-aggressive blindness is counterproductive, to say the least. Interacting with them leaves a bad taste. Temper tantrums, pouting, and cold shoulders have a way of thinning out the crowd.

Interest in and respect for the other's point of view is a hallmark of maturity, as is accountability. The immature pass the buck, the mature take responsibility. And that responsibility factors in the domino effect of decision making. "No man is an island" runs counter to "my way or the highway." The mature person acknowledges the needs and contributions of those about them. If there's conflict or misunderstanding they say "my bad", whereas the self-absorbed defensively say, "not my fault." Their blame-shifting is the stuff of playgrounds. Taking ownership is beyond their depth.

The maturity component, however, doesn't play in the initial flush of falling in love. One is blindsided by the flood of feelings. And a major ingredient in that emotional tsunami is novelty. Newness is beguiling. One feels fully alive "when the juices are flowing." Inevitably, however, the feelings fade, and the juices thicken and congeal. What does one do then? The apparent loss of love is confusing, if not crushing. The thing about novelty is that it is full of promise. New possibilities, new horizons, new adventures, new beginnings. Indeed, it's like an ocean tide of hope. It temporarily blinds the love-struck to reality, which makes the downside of falling in love (crashing down to earth) all the crueler. And, as Peggy Lee beautifully and mournfully sang, *"If that's all there is, my friend, then let's keep dancing. Let's break out the booze and have a ball... if that's all there is..."*

Fortunately those waves of emotion are *not* all there is. Beneath the breakers are deeper waters of intellect and will. Love is three-dimensional. The brain kicks into gear with what my grandmother used to describe as "giving your head a shake."

Engaging your mind can involve reading, studying, learning from experience, and listening to wise friends and relatives. In so doing you'll discover that love is a number of things. In no particular order, here are a few descriptors of what love is:

## Reciprocal

Mutuality, of course, is a given. We're not talking self-love here, but love for another. And that other is a real person, someone with a gene-pool, a family history, likes and dislikes, strengths and weaknesses, good moods and bad, truly a universe in herself. She's no cipher, but a living, breathing being who deserves your respect. And, hopefully, she sees you the same way.

## Romantic

As already noted, feelings come and go, but they are key components in lasting love.

Sometimes when they're on the wane all you need is a little romance to rekindle the fire. You may not feel like it but you can intentionally create an atmosphere (on a long walk, a special dinner, a surprise adventure) where she feels special and pampered. Moments like these will nurture your love with wonder, mystery, and memory, On occasion, many years in the future, she will say, with light in her eyes, "Remember when..." Ongoing affirmation is *always* a plus. Remember that the polar opposite of romance is indifference.

## Affectionate

Whereas romance sometimes has to be planned, affection is spontaneous. This is where hugs and kisses come in, not as prelude to the bedroom, but simply as "I'm besotted with you! I'm so glad you're in my life! Gee you're beautiful!" Moments like these will fuel the heart throughout the day. And when you're walking together, hold her hand. Kindness is very bonding.

## Compassionate

Lifelong love brings with it the "slings and arrows of outrageous fortune" as Shakespeare put it in "Hamlet". He strongly questions any effort to end "a sea of troubles" merely by opposing them (Act 3, Sc.1). Many of the troubles of married life are not self-imposed but come our way via illness, unexpected financial reversals, extended family drama, and even natural disasters. And, sometimes the issues are rooted in childhood trauma. This is why a wise husband will be compassionate, showing understanding (perhaps mercy) and thoughtful care in the midst of various crises. Compassion is selflessness in action. It assures her that "you have her back."

## Morally Integral

I once read a story about a young man during the Middle Ages who was brought before the village parson for judgement. They were charging him with adultery. In those days the parson was the "Parson" (*the* person) in that

> *When facing a moral choice you've already decided what you'll do: you'll do the right thing.*

he usually was the only literate person in the community. As such he acted as lawyer, notary, and judge. He asked the young man if the charges were true.

"Yes, Parson," he answered "but you have no idea of the outside pressure I was under."

"Outside pressure? Outside pressure?! Boy, where were your inside braces?"

Sustainable and sustaining love has a strong moral compass. You determine there are roads you *won't* follow, paths you *won't* walk, regardless of the beguilement. When facing a moral choice you've already decided what you'll do: you'll do the right thing. Period. A husband with a moral backbone of steel will always be his sweetheart's hero.

## Peaceful

The Oxford English Dictionary refers to "at peace" as "a state of friendliness." What a concept! Your spouse as your friend! We are graceful, uplifting, respectful, truthful, and good-humored with our friends. These characteristics go hand in glove with peace. There is a serenity that pervades a friendly home where mutual respect, thoughtful affirmation and transparency prevail. Best friends have a long shelf-life.

## Forgiving

Forgiveness is huge. Whole books have been written about it. Questions like "How often do I forgive?", "When?", "If I forgive am I endorsing bad behavior?", "Does forgiving mean forgetting?" occur to all of us when we've been "sinned against." We're all conflicted in this area.

I think forgiveness is something everyone needs on occasion. We remember the relief. But, and this is a big "but", there's no relief if there's no remorse. Sometimes people ask to be forgiven merely as a way of avoiding responsibility for their actions. They're not truly sorry, just cornered. For sure they'll do it again, so forgiving them in their serial offences becomes co-dependency. I've sometimes said to women, "If he hits you once and asks for forgiveness, grant it. If he hits you again, call the cops." Sounds harsh because it is.

Forgiveness does *not* mean forgetting. But it does free us from marinating in the memory for the rest of our lives. It's much better to look forward. Nevertheless, for forgiveness to work there has to be at least one adult in the room.

## Faithful

A loving husband is trustworthy, constant, and unwavering in his commitment to and care for his wife. To use a word seldom seen these days, he is "steadfast" in love. This is why his wife believes in him. She too, in her faithfulness, is unwavering in her commitment, so it can be truly said, "They believe in each other." Faithfulness feeds belief and belief feeds faithfulness (more about this in a later chapter.) Little wonder their marriage is as solid as a rock. On such a foundation they both feel secure, confident and content.

These few characteristics of lasting love, obvious as they are, often are off the radar of the eager male. Rather than think about what I call "the business of loving," he chooses to think with his "other brain", the one that seeks the bedroom. Relationship for him means sex, not life. He needs to think with his "big brain", keeping in mind that what you think is what you are.

Many years ago I was invited to speak to a senior high-school class about sex. I had just initiated a phone-in talk show for teenagers on the city's number one rock radio station, and the first program created quite a stir. I called it "Sex and the Single Student." I wasn't sure if the invitation was intended to disparage or to encourage me, but I went "into the jaws of the lions" fully prepared to bear the consequences. I hoped I'd be able to add value in some way.

The class went well until I began to talk about the potential downside of premarital sex. One of the guys interrupted with an angry, "What! You don't buy a car without a test drive! You gotta try her out!" Bellows of male laughter and embarrassed groans from the girls quickly subsided to stone silence. They became a captive audience as I said, "So fella, a girl is like a car huh? You grade her on looks and performance. You drive her hard and then trade her in on a newer model? She's nothing but a ride." I said a lot more, but the gauge of my impact was evident as the class dismissed. The boys slunk away, while the girls stayed to talk. The teacher finally had to send them out to avoid missing their next class. "There's no way I'll ever date *that* guy!" one of them stated as she left the classroom. I did, however, overhear another girl say as she walked away, "I wouldn't mind test-driving a few guys myself." I guess sex as recreation cuts both ways. Nevertheless, a rocky relational road awaits those whose gonads do the thinking.

You don't have to be a rocket scientist to think about sex in terms of its short and long-term ramifications. Indeed, engaging our brain can have remarkable impact. Like anything else in life that is worthwhile, sooner or later (hopefully sooner) you've got to think it through.

In ancient cultures sex was not sexualized, as it is today. It was less about recreation and more about procreation. Sons were indispensable in preserving the father's name and lineage. Tribal integrity and longevity depended on it. Every child born was born to a clan or community that hailed its arrival. And, because sex was so closely allied with daily survival, any abuse or perversion was anathema. There always were moral aberrations, of course, but they were seen as a threat to lineal continuity and were dealt with harshly. Because when you get right down to it, sex is about *life*. It was/is utterly vital to the sustainability of humankind.

So, regardless of ancient or modern culture, engaging the mind about sex means, at least, the recognition that it isn't a game, recreation, or sport. If it is seen as mere conquest it quickly sours. The only meaning it brings, ultimately, is in faithful love and family. Sex is not just *about* life, it is *for* life. That's why it's called "making love". And the experts tell us the "making" is not the work of our nether regions, rather it is brain-work. You've probably read that the brain is our number one sex organ. Our hormones must ultimately bow to our brain cells.

> *The brain is our number one sex organ. Our hormones must ultimately bow to our brain cells.*

Those "little grey cells", as Agatha Christie's Hercule Poirot puts it, are inextricably tied to our decision making. In the final analysis love is what you do. It's all about action. The history and legacy of our lives is the inviolable product of our decisions in the day to day cut and thrust of existence. We live and we love choice by choice. We feel, we think, and we do.

The "doing" is where the rubber meets the road. As the lyric in "My Fair Lady" puts it, *"Don't talk of stars burning above, if you're in love show me... Don't talk of June, don't talk of Fall, don't talk at all, show me."* As some anonymous bard put it, "Talk is cheap."

Decision-making is easy for some, hard for others. Some decide quickly (sometimes too quickly), and some decide slowly. Some have difficulty deciding at all (which in itself is a decision). Regardless, our will must be engaged. Ultimately, "I love you" is a call to action.

The fundamental impetus in loving a woman for life is to add value. You are committed to seeking her highest good. To all intents and purposes her interests take priority. "Whoa!" you say. "That's a bit much!" Indeed it is. But it's the only way to a sustainable relationship.

This doesn't mean you're a doormat. You're not her slave, obligated to fulfil her every whim. You're a partner, and you decide to add value in a mutual context of transparent communication. You've got to listen to her, and she to you. No assumptions. Just clear, honest talk. Openness is vital – it shows the way forward. And it's good to take the initiative, even if it's just a simple, "So, how was your day?" And never forget the followup questions. Shows you're listening.

Communication, however, is merely the starting point. The perspective, the needs, the joys, and the sorrows should be catalysts to both strategic and tactical performance. A course must be set with the short term and the long term in view. You must be friend, lover, caregiver, defender, provider, comforter, and confidant, a faithful multi-tasker who does what he does not out of duty alone, but for the joy of having this woman in his life.

The great thing about love is that you can decide to add value even when you don't feel like it. Decisions trump feelings. For example, you had a bad day at work, you fought with the boss, and on the way home you rehearsed the arguments. Now, as you approach your home, you're still in a fighting mood. As you open the door she calls from the kitchen, "Hi Sweetie! Did you pick up the dry cleaning?" Rats! You forgot. And now you remember she needs that outfit for the dinner party at her obnoxious cousin's house. You don't want to go. You want to snap. Lashing out, of course, will put her on the defensive and set a tone for the night. So... "Oops, I forgot. I'll go now. Back in five. I know you need that dress for tonight. I'm sure you're looking forward to seeing Jenny again...". You keep your upset to yourself, and, surprisingly, the evening goes quite well. Your decision to love won.

So, whether major or minor, your tone and your action adds another page to your love story. We're all writing a book our children and grandchildren will read one day. We want it to be a good read. This, however, does not mean we're perfect wordsmiths. Many times we get it wrong. As the old British expression puts it, sometimes we "blot our copybook". We blow it. When we do, the most loving thing is to admit it and say "Sorry. My bad." There are very few wives who will reject a heartfelt confession. The unspoken expectation is that you will discipline yourself next time.

Self-discipline is key in lasting love. Indiscipline stresses the flow of day-to-day relationship, rather like an out of balance tire on your car. You feel the vibration with every rotation – if not corrected it will eventually break down. Sometimes the wheel will detach with sorrowful consequences. Just a small bit of counter-balance (self-discipline) makes for a smooth ride. Self-awareness is the place to start.

It's simple: you've got to know yourself. Then again, maybe it's not so simple. Self-awareness demands maturity, which means, among other things, that you can look at yourself objectively. It's called being an adult.

The Oxford dictionary defines maturity in terms of "fully developed powers of mind and body." This suggests incremental growth via time, experience, education, and intentional appropriation of core values. It's the gradual replacement of instant gratification with impulse control, and vision for the future. The subjective yields to the objective. "What's in it for me?" in the context of lasting love is eclipsed by "What's in it for us?" Maturity respects and submits to mutuality.

So, you look at yourself and what do you see? Maybe the answers to three- basic questions will help:

1 Who am I?
2 What/where do I want to be?
3 How will I get there?

> To grow up means to "man-up".

This is not a pseudo-psychological quiz. There are no right answers, rather they're *your* answers. Who? What/Where? And How? reveal the internal braces of your person and character. They uncover your worldview. You may or may not like all that you see. To grow up means to "man-up".

Maybe you draw a blank. You have no answers. What do I do now! I can't find my internal, let alone moral, compass. I'm lost. Do I need a shrink?

No, you don't need counselling, you need to take stock. You may still be young, but you've been (and are) leaving a legacy. If you were to die today what would you be remembered for? Too many memorials sentimentalize unrealized potential in those who pass with saccharine tributes such as, "He was always smiling. He was such a good guy. He never hurt anyone. He was always there for me..." When, in fact, people hardly saw him. He spent hours each day playing video games in his parents' basement. His legacy is laziness and lassitude. He was not a contributor, he was a consumer. His departure leaves little or no vacuum, regardless of the bromides.

Taking stock starts with that simple but brutal question: Am I a consumer or a contributor? Children consume, adults contribute. If, in a protracted adolescent way, you are still controlled by your appetites, your current girlfriend (and future wife?) is merely an object. On the other hand, if you're maturing and taking responsibility for your choices she's a person. You're looking, adult-to-adult, to merging your trajectories. Those who take the line of least resistance and merely "settle" ("She'll do"... "He'll do") won't be settled for long. But those who truly love each other are off on a life-long adventure. They'll always feel their love but they'll fuel it with their choices. And you, my dear husband (or husband-to-be), would be wise to set the tone.

## FOUR

# Be Faithful

"In Memoriam A.H.H.," is touted as one of the greatest poems of the 19th century. Written by Alfred Lord Tennyson, Britain's poet laureate during Queen Victoria's reign, it's a funeral requiem for his good friend, Arthur Henry Hallam who died at the young age of 22 while a student at Cambridge. Victoria said this poem brought her great comfort on the passing of her much loved husband, Prince Albert. There are so many quotable stanzas. For example:

*"Ring out the want, the care, the sin,*
*the faithless coldness of the times;*
*Ring out, ring out my mournful rhymes,*
*But ring the fuller minstrel in.*

*Ring out false pride in place and blood.*
*The civic slander and the spite;*

*Ring in the love of truth and right,*
*Ring in the common love of good.*
*Ring out old shapes of foul disease;*
*Ring out the narrowing lust of gold;*
*Ring in the thousand years of peace.*

*Ring in the valiant man and free,*
*The larger heart, the kindlier hand;*
*Ring out the darkness of the land;*
*Ring in the Christ that is to be."*

IN MEMORIAM A.H.H. (1850) CANTO 106

No doubt Tennyson was in a bleak mood as he penned these words. The sorrowful loss of A.H.H. exacerbated a dim view of the world. He writes of "the faithless coldness of the times" and describes that coldness in terms of "want, care, sin, false pride, slander, spite, disease, lust (greed), war, and darkness." The key descriptor is faithless.

The converse of "faithless", of course, is "faithful", not just in terms of belief in something bigger than yourself, but also in terms of behavior consistent with the belief and trust shown in you by others. Faithfulness is truth in action ("the love of truth and right"), and seeks to do and be good ("the common love of good"). It produces "valiant... and free" souls with "larger" and "kindlier" hearts. Indeed, it creates "the fuller minstrel". The "coldness" and "darkness" yield to warmth and light.

Usually, in the context of marriage, faithfulness is seen as "keeping thee only unto her as long as ye both shall live" (from the classic marriage vows), which we interpret as "no cheating". That's a no-brainer. But there is so much more to faithfulness than exclusive sexual devotion. It covers the entire range of our character and behavioral life. It's a huge subject. Let's try for a brief summary, starting with a short anecdote:

My young wife and I had just taken our first-born child home from the hospital. Worn out, the new mom had a nap while I carried the well-bundled baby out for a walk through our neigborhood. I was besotted. Looking at this little miracle in my arms I wasn't watching my step. Suddenly I tripped, lost my balance and tumbled to the ground. Instantly the "barrel roll" technique I'd learned in football kicked into gear. Holding my son to my chest, I rolled onto my back and up to my feet. The little guy didn't even wake up. He was safe in his father's arms.

A faithfully loved woman feels safe in her husband's arms. There is certainty, the foundation is firm, he is trustworthy. He will not let her fall.

That relational certainty exists not just because he follows through in his commitment to her, but also because he himself is firmly established in terms of his character and "inside braces". As such he is totally dependable. To him "till death do us part" is marching orders. He's in it for the long haul.

Contrast this with that hormonal highschooler who just wants to "test-drive the car". He's looking for a ride. The faithful husband, on the other hand, wants a life. And, ultimately life wins, whether for good or for bad. Unfaithfulness delaminates life whereas faithfulness produces three-dimensional joy. Too many unhappy, disaffected, bitter old men have lives littered with broken promises. In the end their relational shallowness sees them dislocated and alone. He may still be married, not physically alone, but spiritually and emotionally a solitary soul living with a long-suffering woman orphaned by indifference.

> *Unfaithfulness delaminates life whereas faithfulness produces three-dimensional joy.*

None of us knows the universe we're falling into when we fall in love. Earlier in the book I've suggested some of the best and worse-case scenarios that may be hidden beneath the surface of that beguiling other. Again, referencing those classic vows, "for better or for worse" calls for future faithfulness that may test the outer limits of that covenant. What if she cheats on you? What if an operation disfigures her? What if she battles with mental illness? What will you do then? Will you bail out (as many men do) or will you dig deep? Will you be as faithful to her sick bed as you were to your marriage bed? Will you be as constant in crisis as you have been in the good times? Now is the time to decide that if and when the worst happens you'll do what is right. Duty demands it.

Faithfulness is dutiful. It takes responsibility on a daily basis. It knows that love, like life, doesn't just happen, it takes work. Nevertheless, duty does not necessarily mean drudgery. Maybe you've heard or read the well-worn adage, "If you work at what you love, you'll never work a day in your life." And, if you work at loving the one you love, you'll never live a day in your life unloved. Love is reciprocal. As the famous originator of psychoanalysis, Sigmund Freud, put it, "all that matters is love and work."

Another key component in faithfulness is integrity. In the very core of your soul you must be convinced of and dedicated to your commitments. When you tell her you love her you've got to mean it. It is not merely a transaction, it is a covenant, a hill you will die on if necessary. Otherwise you're a hypocrite claiming to love someone you don't love, with perhaps just time and circumstance standing between you and infidelity.

Faithful commitment is the foundation of morality. You choose to honor your commitments rather than indulge your appetites. One of the most common laments from women disappointed with love is, "He just won't commit." Why he won't is often the result of immaturity, lack of impulse control, limited vision for his life, and a desire to pick every flower in the garden. He's easily distracted, easily beguiled, easily seduced. He wants "to have it all." His word is not his bond. He's gone AWOL.

There are any number of examples I could draw on of husbands who were not AWOL. Let me tell you about a friend, Dave, and his wife, Gloria.

Dave was a young single man of twenty-seven years when he moved to the northern Ontario city where my father was pastoring. He was tall, handsome, and shy. An expert heavy equipment mechanic he had been promoted by the Ministry of Transportation to the role of "mechanic supervisor", overseeing several mechanics who maintained Ontario's fleet of trucks in the region. He did his job well.

Shortly after his arrival in town he made an appointment to see my dad. He wanted to attend our church. Plus, he knew of dad's reputation as a wise and caring pastor, and wanted to get his counsel re: finding a wife. "I don't just want to settle for a girl," he said, "I want someone who'll take my breath away." This was a brave statement from a guy so shy he had a hard time looking any woman in the eye. "I also looked for a beauty," said Dad, "and I'm glad I did" (my mom was gorgeous). There was the predictable talk of character and virtue of course, but my father reiterated what he had said to me on one occasion, "You want a good and beautiful woman looking at you across the breakfast table every morning, son. It makes the journey well worth it." Dad did in marriage what he did in everything else – he practised what he preached.

It took a few years before Dave found the stunning Gloria. During that time he continued to work hard, attend church faithfully, and pursue his love of hunting and fishing. He used to take me (12 years his junior) occasionally to his favorite fishing hole to catch small mouth bass. We had to walk a mile from a logging road to a hidden pond up and over several rocky hills. The first time we went he warned me that the footing was treacherous along one of the slopes. "Let me lead you," he said, and immediately lost his footing and unceremoniously slid down into a swamp. Laughing uproariously I dubbed him "Fearless leader!", and that became his moniker for as long as I knew him. A few decades later I happened to see him across the foyer of a church at a funeral. I called out, "Hey, Fearless Leader!", and he turned with a huge smile, taking up where we'd left off years ago. Friends are like that, no?

When Dave started dating Gloria there were more than a few wags in our church rolling their eyes wondering what she saw in this semi-reclusive guy. "He's good looking," I heard one whisper to another "but he's so shy! No personality, She'll be bored in no time...". What they didn't (couldn't) know was that once Dave's breath had been taken away he would put a full court press on winning and keeping Gloria's heart. And he did, for 58 years! His secret? Total devotion and tireless faithfulness.

Eighteen years into their marriage Gloria developed a serious auto-immune disease. In a matter of months she was incapacitated. She couldn't walk, dress herself, go to the bathroom. She became fully invalid. Dave took it in stride. He became her care-giver. He made sure she was looked after by an in-house assistant while he was at work, but when he was home each night and on weekends he was her everything. It was as though Gloria wasn't even sick. They talked, laughed, watched movies on tv, went out, attended church, gathered with friends. As he pushed Gloria about in her wheelchair (which he called her "freedom machine") he looked and acted happy. So did she, because they were. The medications and steroids drastically altered her appearance but her smile was radiant (How can you not radiate joy when you love and are loved?). Gloria recovered some of her mobility over the next forty years, but Dave was her strength. He pushed, she rode, they had fun right up until Dave's death at 85 years of age.

Faithful love is like mountain air. It oxygenates the soul. It's like a fountain of youth. It is timeless and energizing. Little wonder that a couple married faithfully for decades knows happiness that younger people can only aspire to. Like the best of wines a loving marriage matures into perfection as it ages. More time, more better. More love, more joy.

> *Like the best of wines a loving marriage matures into perfection as it ages. More time, more better.*

To this point in the chapter I could be faulted with being a touch idealistic, and a bit too "wise". I think of Rudyard Kipling's classic poem "IF" and his caution that we "don't look too good, nor talk too wise..." This kind of smugness is to be avoided. I realize that the vast landscape of faithfully loving a woman for life is far beyond any attempt to capture in one painting. Indeed, much of lasting husbandry is the product of unknown and unexpected circumstance as much as it is of intentional technique. Character can inform but often trumps strategy.

You can Google "IF", but let me quote it for you:

> *"If you can keep your head when all about you*
> *Are losing theirs and blaming it on you;*
> *If you can trust your self when all men doubt you,*
> *But make allowance for their doubting too;*
> *If you can wait and not be tired by waiting,*
> *Or being lied about, don't deal in lies,*
> *Or, being hated, don't give way to hating,*
> *And yet don't look too good, nor talk too wise;*

## BE FAITHFUL

*If you can dream – and not make dreams your master;*
    *If you can think – and not make thoughts your aim;*
*If you can meet with triumph and disaster*
    *And treat those two imposters just the same;*
*If you can bear to hear the truth you've spoken*
    *Twisted by knaves to make a trap for fools,*
*Or watch the things you gave your life to broken,*
    *And stoop and build 'em up with worn-out tools;*

*If you can make one heap of all your winnings*
    *And risk it on one turn of pitch-and-toss,*
*And lose, and start again at your beginnings*
    *And never breathe a word about your loss;*
*If you can force your heart and nerve and sinew*
    *To serve your turn long after they are gone,*
*And so hold on when there is nothing in you*
    *Except the Will which says to them: "Hold on";*

*If you can talk with crowds and keep your virtue,*
    *Or walk with kings – nor lose the common touch;*
*If neither foes nor loving friends can hurt you;*
    *If all men count with you, but none too much;*
*If you can fill the unforgiving minute*
    *With sixty seconds' worth of distance run –*
*Yours is the Earth and everything that's in it,*
    *And – which is more – you'll be a Man, my son!"*

This is not an "English Literature 101" class, so I won't be too analytical. But as I read "IF" I see at least twelve character traits that contribute greatly to a man's capacity to be a faithful, loving husband. I'll identify them without "quoting chapter and verse" (you can do that spade work). According to Kipling we boys grow into men by being:

## 1. Objective

It's good to step back from the stress of accident, failure, panic, and blame-shifting to get the "2000-foot view" of what's really going on. Especially when you are the one being accused for the upset, you need to temper any defensive reflex and be clear thinking and measured in your assessment and response to the situation.

## 2. Self-confident

I know. I can hear you saying, "Easier said than done!" Entire books, masters and doctorate degrees, and endless counselling sessions revolve around this topic. But I like Kipling's succinct focus on two things, one positive, the other negative: a) trust yourself, b) distrust the opinions of others. As Polonius said to Laertes in Shakespeare's "Hamlet" (Act 1, Scene 3) – "This above all: to thine own self be true. And it must follow, as the night the day Thou canst not then be false to any man...".

Trusting yourself provides the solid footing upon which to build both a life and a marriage.

## 3. Patient

The Oxford Dictionary defines patience as "calm endurance for hardship, provocation, pain, delay... tolerant perseverance or forbearance... the capacity for calm self-possessed waiting." An impatient person sees the trying situation as a personal affront – "that car is holding *me* up!" (and potential road rage rears its ugly head). Impulse control issues are a constant in the lives of impatient people. They want instant gratification. They can't back off. They want to shoulder through. Get out of *my* way! This of course is counter-productive in life, let alone in marriage. Patience makes way for the other's perspective. It allows for mitigating circumstances. It chills.

## 4. Honest

Richard Whately, English philosopher and theologian (1787 – 1863), also Archbishop of Dublin in 1831, once famously wrote, "Honesty is the best policy; but he who is governed by that maxim is not an honest man." In other words, one can talk honesty and not live honestly. We can claim to be telling the truth even as we are untrue. Maybe this was at the root of the timeless question Pilate, the Roman procurator who ordered Jesus' crucifixion, posed, "What is truth?" It can be bent in any direction we choose.

Having acknowledged humankind's predisposition to lying, we still value unblemished truth-telling, that is, truth in practise. Our actions witness to our integrity. A lie, even under the guise of "frankly speaking", is like a weed. It grows fast and proliferates other weeds. The truth, on the other hand, is like a mighty oak – it grows straight and true, and stands the test of time.

## 5. Humble

Humility, like honesty, can be faked. False humility is common, but there can be a subtler deception: self-deprecation. Putting oneself down is often an aggressive egoism in that it is searching for praise and affirmation even if it means verbal grovelling to get it. Sometimes (an even more subtle subtlety) self-deprecation is preemptive – "I'll put myself down before they do...". The fact is that humility has little to do with one's self image. The ancient Greeks and Hebrews saw it as malleability, willingness to be shaped, openness to learning. A humble soul was a work in progress. So one could be self-confident and humble at the same time. Indeed, it could be argued that humility reflects a position of strength. Strong character is always open to correction.

## 6. Active

Kipling knows that a young man has many dreams and ideas. These can culminate in vision, an absolutely vital component in character. But he warns against passivity. Ultimately one must be a doer, not just a thinker or a dreamer. Sexual fantasies are a sort of superficial, self-focused dreaming. These can be powerful and persistent, reaching far beyond their beginnings in adolescence into adulthood. Too often pornography fuels these flames, but it is inferior fuel, rather like straw – it bursts into explosive heat for a moment, quickly expires, and must be replaced with more straw. You have to keep feeding these short-lived flames with more and more and more, but it's never enough. There is no sustainability, no satisfaction, just emptiness and self-disgust, and eventual sexual death. Ironically, pornography is passive, a witness to weakness.

> *Ironically, pornography is passive, a witness to weakness.*

The English poet John Donne (1572 – 1631) struck a chord when he wrote,

> *"Dear love, for nothing less than thee*
> *Would I have broke this happy dream,*
> *It was a theme*
> *For reason, much too strong for fantasy."*

SONGS AND SONNETS – THE DREAM

Being sexually active in marriage is strong drink. It requires much more than mere fantasy or even desire. It is intentional, it is other-focused (your wife's needs before yours) as it gives before it takes. The real world is its arena. The novelist, Iris Murdock (1919 – 1999) put it this way, "We live in a fantasy world, a world of illusion. The great task in life is to find reality." We've got to get our heads out of the clouds and get our feet on the ground, marching to the beat of making a life.

## 7. Graceful

There are a number of ways to describe "grace". The most common being that of showing goodwill or favor to someone, even though it may be undeserved (sometimes that someone may be you yourself). The common meaning of grace in ancient Greek was "pleasantness" or "attractiveness". In that sense to be "graceful" is to be pleasing and engaging, with the predisposition to seek for and find the same qualities in others. It is a gracious thing to see the good beyond the bad. Your Aunt Mabel understood this when she told you, "If you can't say something good about a person, say nothing at all." Grace carries a lot of weight in sustainable marriage. It creates a positive atmosphere in your home. It lets the soul breathe freely, whereas un-grace sees a relationship gasping. Kipling encourages his son to be graceful in both victory and defeat, understanding that both polarities are temporary. He also suggests that being misrepresented or misunderstood has a brief shelf-life. Avoid defensiveness and be the adult in the room. Grace provides equilibrium.

## 8. Resilient

A few years ago I was felling trees on a heavily wooded property. It was an old growth forest that needed some pruning before we could build a little cabin "off the grid", as they say. We wanted to provide room for a few promising saplings to grow as well.

To my chagrin one of the tall trees I felled crashed down over a beautiful young maple, crushing it to the ground. It was several hours of "bucking" with my chainsaw before I could free the young tree. I expected it to be broken beyond repair. Immediately upon its release the sapling, to my amazement, slowly sprang back to its former vertical. It was like watching a time lapse movie. How resilient!

"Resilient" means to "recoil" or "spring back, resuming its original shape after bending" (Oxford Dictionary). It "readily recovers from shock, depression, etc." Thomas More (1478 - 1535), Lord High Chancellor of England under King Henry VIII is credited (among a few others) with the well-worn quote, "I'll lay me down and bleed awhile, and then I'll rise and fight again." Whether it's suffering slander, broken dreams, shattered accomplishments, or risks gone bad, Kipling calls on his son to rise again without self-pity or complaint. Whining in life, let alone in marriage, is bad form.

## 9. Strong

We're not talking muscle-power here. We're talking will-power. Some physically unintimidating people have been powerful world changers – think Joan of Arc or Napoleon. Their's was not strength of body but of will. The application is clear: "This is the woman I will love. I will love no other. Ever." Your "heart and nerve and sinew" are hers "until death do us part."

## 10. Consistent

There are many nuances to "consistency" but consider that strength of character which enables you to think clearly before you conform to social convention or expectation. This is not to suggest you be a Luddite (opposing something new), but knowing what your core values are, and sticking to them, will see you acting consistently through life. We know that what was "politically correct" in the 20th Century is not necessarily so in the 21st. Social values and mores are as inconsistent as cloud patterns. If you tie yourself to what's current you'll be just as scattered. This is not a call to being reactive, but to proactivity (leading rather than following). It will see you pursuing a clear horizon rather than stumbling about in the dust-trail of social convention.

Recently a medical professional asked me how long I'd been married. When I answered, "Fifty years," she exclaimed, "Fifty years?! In my world that's *five* marriages!" In a society that increasingly marries (if marries at all) with the back door open, it's little wonder that divorce is the norm. So, buck the trend and marry for life.

## 11. Thick-skinned

Toughness is a corollary to strength. Taking things personally is counter-productive. There are always going to be insults, slights, and bruises, all the more hurtful when it's not just "foes" but "loving friends" who hurt you. We have a choice: let the blow bounce off, or assume a fetal position and simmer in the wounds. As my grandmother used to say, "Better to be better than bitter." Roll with it and get on with living. Marriage is a journey, not a destination.

## 12. Purposeful

Once again consulting my trusty Oxford Dictionary I find four definitions for "purpose":

1. an object to be attained; a thing intended; 2. the intent to act; 3. resolution, determination; 4. the reason for which something is done or made. Thus, a purposeful person is someone "having or indicating purpose." They are "intentional, resolute". They know where they're going and will doggedly pursue the course come what may. It's a no-brainer. A man who faithfully pursues, performs, and protects his love for his wife will have a happy marriage. "The love of truth and right" will see you through.

FIVE

# Lust, Adultery & Divorce

If you're human you know what lust is. No need for me to define it, nor will I speak ill of it. The passion and hunger we feel for physical pleasure, connection, and (dare I say it?) procreation, is as real as our daily need for food, water and sleep. There's something innate in human nature that whether we're atheist or true believer we want to follow through on the first command God gave mankind, "Be fruitful, and multiply...". We're very willing, eager even (!), to have sex. As author C. S. Lewis put it, most of us men are ready "to populate a small village."

My first awareness of sex is dim. I was only three years of age. Dad was pastoring a small country church in Alberta. The building was small with an uninsulated "parsonage" attached at the back. There was only one bedroom. So my brother and I slept on little mattresses within arms length of our parents. I woke one night to sounds from their bed. I squinted in the darkness to see my dad wrestling with my mother – at least that's how it looked. This alarming behavior continued for a bit and then it ended. I heard some contented cooing from Mom so my alarm gave way and I went back to sleep. At three I didn't have the critical faculties to ask Why? or What's up with that? It didn't occur to me that my very existence began with a similar tussle. Indeed, your story began with sex too.

Most of us refer to intercourse as "making love" when we know that satisfying a hunger can be all about ourselves. The hunger (the "lust") has to be for more than release of sexual tension, it must also be for connecting and pleasuring someone we love. This altruism sees selfish, "coital masturbation" (as I've read it described), yield to focus on the other. One's self is absorbed in a powerful union which, of course, is the only sex that has a long shelf-life. When sex is all about her you are truly making love, love for a lifetime.

> *When hormones take the lead love will ultimately fail, but where love is in the lead hormones follow.*

Love, unlike hormones, is not subject to the law of diminishing returns. When hormones take the lead love will ultimately fail, but where love is in the lead hormones follow. After more than fifty years of marriage I bear witness to this truth! This, of course, is counter-cultural in our relationally hungry world. Yet the grim reality of our western sexual freedoms is an increasing dissatisfaction with sex, evidence that hormonal drive has a thin veneer. A recent demonstration in a major American university saw young students marching for asexuality. One poster stood out: "How 'Bout We Just Cuddle? Asexual and Proud." For many women cuddling trumps orgasm. Being held is a greater value than being penetrated. Not only does it release those "cooing" endorphins but it engages the heart.

Years ago I attended a farming exposition at a small mid-western town. Farmers from the region had their products on display, as did the farm equipment manufacturers. It was a festival atmosphere. As I entered one of the exhibition barns I saw a long line of heifers tied to their stalls. There were about twenty of them, docilely chewing their cud. But halfway down the row of well groomed cattle I saw what looked like a cow having an epileptic fit. It was heaving, yanking at its tether, kicking, and bawling. I even saw spittle flying. I rushed down the line to see what this cow's problem was. Turned out it wasn't a cow at all. It was a bull, fully frustrated that he was flanked by a harem of beauties that couldn't be serviced. Poor guy! Most of us men can feel his pain. Some of us break the tether.

Men often see that tether as marriage. To mix metaphors many are like a famous French crooner who rationalized his womanizing as wanting "to pick every flower in the garden." And, as we know from our own neighborhoods, let alone the media, there are a lot of flowers for the picking. Exciting no? Then again, maybe not. I hear the Rolling Stones singing in the background, "I can't get no satisfaction...". Infidelity leaves a sour taste.

When we cheat we know it's wrong. Like the singer we rationalize ("I wasn't getting enough from my wife") and we negotiate with our conscience. We try to do an end run around guilt. We come up with all kinds of excuses, but there is no excuse for making a choice. We're free to choose, and choose we do. The sticky thing about choices is that there's no remaking them. Like words spoken that are never forgotten, an affair, fling, or one night stand, will always darken your wife's soul, even if she forgives you. It will darken your soul too. A chronic philanderer once told me that he had "left a part of his soul" with every woman he'd slept with. "My soul is pretty much empty," he sadly admitted, "and my wife's soul died years ago...". Statistics tell us that only 15% of marriages survive infidelity. Our culture doesn't like the word "sin", but experience tells us that adultery is certainly a transgression. Perhaps the greatest victim of the act is trust.

Twenty years ago Martin committed adultery. A "corner office" partner in a successful law firm, he was a powerful man surrounded by a coterie of ambitious young lawyers. Several were highly motivated women. One of them was newly married, especially attractive, and seemed to find Martin attractive too. Her name was Brooke.

It all started "innocently" as he reflected years later. He noticed she looked his way a lot when they were in weekly staff meetings. He found himself returning these protracted glances. When issues arose in discussion she often defended his views and seemed genuinely concerned about him. She began to arrive at these meetings a few minutes early, not just to exchange pleasantries, but to take the chair beside him at the table. Occasionally her knee brushed against his, and sometimes the contact was sustained. This out-of-sight intimacy was arousing.

Brooke began coming to his office regularly with items of business that needed attention – these were innocuous, legitimate reasons to be alone together. The door, of course, was always open. As they sat together the chemistry was intoxicating. All the ingredients for adultery were there. They only had to mix and stir, put it on the burner and turn up the heat. Simmer soon became boil.

> *All the ingredients for adultery were there. They only had to mix and stir, put it on the burner and turn up the heat.*

A few business luncheons stoked the fire. Then on a flight together to an important contract signing with a key partner they talked and touched without reserve. Two hotel rooms, connected by an access door, became one that night. As did they. His later claim that Brooke "blindsided" him was, of course, not true. He had cultivated her as she did him. It was all so predictable. Adultery is an old story.

It's a story about thoughtless descent into unintended consequences, collateral damage, lies, loss of trust, and regret. Infidelity promises (and often delivers) hot sex at the beginning and produces a gut punch at the end. Like Esau in the book of Genesis, adultery "sells one's birthright for a mess of pottage." It is a lose-lose entanglement.

We might think that the main losers are those who are betrayed. Yet, long before the affair is discovered or revealed the unfaithful pair are the first to suffer. Their humanity (often the excuse – "He's only human you know!") surfaces, not in terms of sex but in terms of moral compass. Most of us are not without conscience. We have brains which do kick into gear at some point. Guilt, fear of exposure and regret, successfully repressed in the first heat of the liaison, begin to surface. Usually these second thoughts emerge as object becomes person – that is, she/he begins over time to reveal themselves. There's an entire universe underneath that beguiling body, likes, dislikes, quirks, mental and emotional baggage, behaviors and moods. All of this is remarkably parallel to the "real persons" who emerged early on in marriage. "Getting married in a fever" sometimes leads to relational headache. The heat begins to cool.

Ironically, as the affair winds down the drama of the domino effect winds up. Martin's wife finds out. She's crushed. As are the kids, extended family, friends, neighbors, and workmates. The wreckage devastates Martin. He sees the sorrow, disappointment, and betrayal in the eyes of those he has loved and it cuts to the heart. Perhaps his most difficult moment comes when he faces his two teen-aged sons. What kills him is not their sorrow and anger, but the loss of trust and respect. Already he senses that they are looking down on him, not in judgement, but in the dislocation of their worldview. Martin is no longer a safe haven. Their father is adrift and so, consequently, are they. Things will never be the same.

The marriage survived, as did the memory. Yes, his wife forgave him, and over two or three years of healing it seemed they had put the affair behind them. But, even now, twenty years later there is still that vestigial presence of betrayal. Her trust in him is walking with a limp.

Many marriages, sadly, do not survive. The loss of trust can cut the legs out from under a marriage and the hurt is often beyond repair. The cheated spouse feels profound grief, a raw wound that defies healing. And as we do with pain in general, the quicker we can be free of it the better. So divorce seems to be the ready pain killer.

Studies tell us that infidelity may be the straw that breaks the camel's back already burdened with things like money problems (a *big* factor), constant fighting, physical/mental health issues, and emotional or physical abuse. These contribute to a multi-layered relational ecosystem requiring fine-tuned surgery, not amputation. But no. Our leg hurts, so cut if off. This is not something we would do to our kids. We'll fight to the death for them, but not for our transgressing spouse. Let them go. Let's get on with life.

Sometimes this is the only option, especially if there has been physical and/or emotional abuse. Those who stay with an abuser empower him. Co-dependency is no way to live. Regardless, divorce is a kind of death. For the severed parties resurrection may be a long way off.

But there *is* life after divorce. Its joy/sorrow mix is ultimately up to us. We choose to marinate in bitterness or regenerate in hope. We can look back or look to the far horizon. We face that fork in the road – disempowered or enthused, darkness or light. Mind you, the pursuit of the far horizon may be uphill for the first few years. Much easier to choose the downhill slope of self-pity.

> *The leopard can change its spots. Love will find a way.*

There's a proverb which says, 'love covers all wrongs'. This is not to say that love covers up, but it has the power to transform transgressions. There are countless stories of reconciliation, stories that recount the redemptive impact of confession, repentance, and forgiveness. The leopard *can* change its spots. Love will find a way.

## SIX

# Be Friends

*"When he (Aristotle) was asked, 'What is a friend?' he said,
'One soul inhabiting two bodies.'"*

DIOGENES LAERTIUS: "LIVES OF PHILOSOPHERS", 2ND C

When asked, very few of us can count our friends on more than one hand. We may have many acquaintances, fellow workers and neighbors, but we have few friends. There are always excuses: not enough time, different orbits, work schedules, etc. But we do feel the social pressure to be accepted and popular. We assume that that affirmation comes from "being everyone's friend." So, when in introspective moments we realize that most of our social relationships are superficial we feel cheated. Why don't I have more friends?

Maybe it's because the Greek philosopher Aristotle was right. We have only one soul to share and that precious possession intuitively knows its worth. Nobody offers their soul on the market. We can trust it with very few. And that's the big word: trust. You may trust your banker with your money, your doctor with your health, your grocer with your food... but who do you trust with your soul? With whom can you share your inmost thoughts, needs, insecurities, and dreams? Only a "soul-mate" will do.

> *Marriage is the perfect petri-dish in which to cultivate the truest of friends.*

Marriage is the perfect petri-dish in which to cultivate the truest of friends. It is where friendship can grow organically. Indeed, friendship in marriage is not a sudden thing, it is a "grown" thing. The initial attraction may provide the seed, but the garden of joy, sorrows, children, memories, and everything else that comprises a home all grow incrementally from day to day. It's a step by step process. Or, at least it *can* be.

For some, unfortunately, it's a step by step erosion with a drip, drip, drip of immaturity, insensitivity, self-centeredness, distrust and indifference. The classic confession of such a marriage is, "We prefer separate vacations." They've become "married singles". And, as amoral as the movie's theme was, they're not even "friends with benefits".

Permanence in marriage is predicated on trust. A trustworthy husband is dependable. His wife has confidence in him. He is true. How important is "true"? Think about it. Would you be sitting comfortably (wherever that might be as you read) if you weren't trusting that the builders of your home knew and practised true measurement and plumb? Because they did your house has stood the test of time. If they hadn't your walls would have collapsed years ago (or maybe you should put the book down right now and check for cracks in the foundation!). Building codes, traffic laws, and our justice system are all standards of the true, and transgressors are held accountable. Without the true we descend into chaos. With the true we live in peace. One might say that trust is a peacemaker.

Friends live in peace. The insecurity and suspicion fuelled by distrust have no home with the peaceful. In the words of the Christmas carol, "Silent Night", "all is calm, all is bright" (at least most of the time). In the absence of that kind of stress a couple can get on with life.

My parents were friends. They met and were engaged during the Second World War, the wedding on hold until my father returned from duty after VE Day. On their wedding day Dad was 23 years old, Mom 18. After a three-day honeymoon they drove their ancient car out to the flat prairies of central Alberta to take on their first pastorate. The church building was located out in the middle of vast farmland, with a treeless 360 degree horizon. The springs were breathtaking with thousands of acres of fast growing wheat rippling like waves in the prevailing winds, the summers were vast-blue-sky beautiful, and the fields of ripened wheat in autumn stunned the senses with magic carpets of gold. The winters? They were something else, freeze your blood scary with temperatures twenty and thirty degrees below zero, biting frost, and blizzards of blowing snow so blinding that it was not uncommon to hear of farmers getting lost between their homes and their barns. On rare occasions they froze to death.

I was born eleven months later, and my brother exactly twelve months (to the day!) after me. We lived in an uninsulated parsonage attached to the humble clapboard church building. Mom used to put us to sleep in winter bundled up in snowsuits, afraid we might freeze to death (she was predisposed to the worse-case scenario for all of her life – too many frozen farmers!). Dad, on the other hand, used to get up twice per night to keep the pot-bellied wood stove stoked. He wasn't as concerned as much about his sons as he was about his wife's peace of mind. His phlegmatic nature counter-balanced her alarmist tendencies. In this and most other ways, they were a perfect match.

I was twenty years old when I left home to go to college. In those two decades I never once saw or heard them fight, let alone argue. There were disagreements and momentary flareups from time to time, but urgency (from Mom) was always met with calm (from Dad). I remember Dad's approach: "Shirl" (he never called her "Dear"), what do you think we should do?"... or, "Here's how I see it, how about you?"... or, "I want you to be happy about this"... or, "You're right, I was wrong" (even if he wasn't)... or, "Let's agree on a solution tomorrow." The words "never" and "always" were absent in any rehearsal of what one or the other had done. There was little fuel for defensive pushback. They were a team.

This was the model with which I was imprinted. And, interestingly, my wife Kathy grew up in the same kind of home. When we married (I at 22 and she at 21 years of age) we both assumed that marriage was more than a partnership – it was a friendship. Now, fifty-two years later, it still is. And, unless I'm suffering long-term memory loss or am guilty of historical revisionism, I can't recount any serious breach in that friendship. Maybe my mom's counsel, "Don't ever go to bed angry" was a key. Any dispute dissolved before dark.

Humor played a huge role in our parents' relationships as it did/does in ours. Baby talk and silly talk (both vocabularies created and fine-tuned when raising our toddlers), seeing the funny side of things, hilarious laughter at ourselves, making faces, playful insults, extemporaneous singing, occasional pranks, and moments of breathless happiness have marked our days. I *love* living with her! And she with me.

Friends share a history. They are persons, not objects or trophies. Indeed, in marriage (with due respect to the experts re: compatibilities) the key to success is companionship. You're not just loving one another, you're *living* with one another. You're sleeping and waking up together, eating and managing household chores together, travelling together, visiting friends and relatives together, and on and on... You are one. "One soul inhabiting two bodies". Two bodies "joined at the hip".

A key component in friendship generally, and marriage specifically, is empathy. Often synonymized with

> *Empathy sees you both walking the same dark road together and embracing the inevitable dawn together.*

sympathy ("to commiserate, condole") empathy has a unique nuance: "the power of identifying oneself mentally with (and so fully comprehending) a person..." (Oxford Dictionary). More than comforting your wife when she's hurting, you truly *feel* her pain. Her hurt is your hurt. You suffer and recover together. Empathy sees you both walking the same dark road together and embracing the inevitable dawn together. Empathy heals.

There will be areas of difficulty where you will find it impossible to truly empathize. Take menstruation for example. This is a time for sympathy. You will need to educate yourself by hearing her when she describes what her period is like and by reading up on the subject. For many women the monthly cycle is almost overwhelming in its hormonal and emotional toll, for others it's a minor inconvenience. You've got to be aware of this. And, as the years pass you'll be wise to learn about peri-menopause and menopause – it's possible that she'll be swimming upstream for many years. A great expression to use again and again is, "Poor baby". Show her you care.

It's critical in these down times to do what you do in the good times: affirm her, again and again. I've stressed this earlier in the book but affirmation is so important I want to stress it once more. The bottom line affirmation, of course, is, "I love you". For over fifty years I've said, "I love you" or "Have I told you lately that I love you?" several times a day. Not once has she rolled her eyes and said, "Enough already!" I don't think there's a wife on the planet who ever tires of being told she's loved. Compliments are welcome too.

Affirmation is more than verbal. Just as non-verbal communication is vital in relationship, so too is non-verbal affirmation. As a child I often saw Dad hugging, kissing, and affectionately stroking Mom's face and hair. He would look her in the eye with warmth and kindness. And, no surprise, she would respond with the same. When they walked anywhere together, they held hands. Two bodies, one soul.

Empathy, sympathy, and affirmation are all part of the larger picture of setting a tone in your marriage. I call this tone-setter "understanding". It's the capacity to think, comprehend, perceive, and make decisions that will add value to your wife's life and warmth to your home. Thinking means having your brain in gear. It's the antithesis of thoughtlessness. As you drive home from work you intentionally imagine what her day has been like. You don't come through the door with, "What's for dinner?" Rather, "Hey sweetie! I'm home. How was your day?" And if she laments you suggest going out for dinner, or ordering in. You've already decided on the drive that she'll be the focus, your number one interest. And, if she gets home from work after you the pattern is the same. "How did it go today? How are you doing? Can I get you a drink? Hey, put up your feet and rest awhile...". You missed her today. Let her know. Set the tone with your tone. Kindness always wins.

There is, of course, much more to understanding. It includes knowledge of where she's coming from in terms of her upbringing. Was she loved as a child? Was she neglected, or worse yet, abused? Did she suffer illness or bereavement? Was she socially accepted? Who were her friends? What were her interests and dreams? Did she battle depression? These are just a few of the questions that can be answered only through open and honest conversation over time. But, with wisdom and restraint (you don't want her to feel intruded upon by your probing) you should be able to get a fair picture of her past. And, in the course of this interaction there will be give and take – she'll learn a lot about you. Self revelation is a two-way street.

This knowledge will give you perceptivity in the day to day dynamics of your relationship. When she speaks or acts in certain ways under stress you'll know what's behind her apparent flare or over-reaction. You'll perceive the thread from her past that attaches to today's drama. You'll be equipped to navigate. And, that skill may require some mid-course correction of your own. We're all flawed no?

Yes, we're all imperfect. So when imperfect marries imperfect we have the potential for a perfect storm. Disaster will follow, sooner or later, unless the love that "conquers all" works its genius. This is the brilliance of love and friendship in marriage: it's the "unconditional" adjective. Let's explore this for a bit.

At the risk of sounding philosophical I think it important to state that before your wife receives your love you've got to be equipped to give it. Trying to give something you don't possess is a zero sum game producing hollowness at home. As they say, "Talk is cheap". A spouse may go to an empty well a few times with hope that the water has returned, but eventually will turn away thirsty. Sometimes that means adultery, separation, and/or divorce. As a husband/friend it's vital to know and acquire the stand-alone (unconditional) qualities whereby you are a loving person (even if you are single all your life). You need to be, and can be, brimming with water. And, to switch metaphors, as one old philosopher put it, "Love is a rope composed of many strands." Light is a spectrum of many colors.

You probably remember your grade school science class about the seven visible spectrum colors of light – red, orange, yellow, green, blue, indigo, and violet. Love has a spectrum too, many more colors than seven. But let me highlight seven:

**1. Patience**

I've often said that the only thing that grows fast in nature is weeds. A lifelong friendship in marriage takes a lifetime to grow. Every year adds another growth ring to your tree. This means that even as you "husband" the tree, with all the intentional thought and activity involved, you also wait. Waiting is hard. It requires mature self-possession. There's no room for immediate gratification, although the incremental development and the adventure of growth will bring satisfaction. Husbanding is fun. But it takes time. Short-temperedness is out. You don't lash out at a tree for its slow growth. You're patient because you have vision.

You see a day of fruitfulness and beauty ahead. The glorious crown of a mature oak is a majestic sight.

## 2. Kindness

> *Kindness is a position of strength.*

Friends are kind to one another. They're gentle and forgiving. Sometimes their kindness seems blind, but friendship sees judgement trumped by generosity of spirit. Harshness is a foreign concept. It speaks of weakness if not of impulse control failure. Kindness is a position of strength. The Australian poet Adam Lindsay Gordon understood this:

> *"Life is mostly froth and bubble,*
> *Two things stand like stone,*
> *Kindness in another's trouble,*
> *Courage in your own."*

YE WEARIE WAYFARER 1866

His linkage of kindness with courage is noteworthy.

## 3. Peacefulness

A peaceful person is tranquil, serene, or as is sometimes said, "in a state of friendliness". An unruffled husband usually has an unruffled wife. Their home is free of strife. It's a happy safe place to live and grow.

Peace is anything but superficial. It has a core deep in a person's soul. To be at peace with oneself is gold. Guilt, regret, injustices and hurts, slights, rejections, disappointments, sorrows, while in process of being resolved and forgotten, have no hold on you. You envy no one, you are respectful, you are malleable and have no self-aggrandizing agenda. You face each morning with a clear conscience. You are free. If you're not there yet (welcome to the human race) remember that freedom is like that oak. It will grow as you tend it. Peace, ironically, is dynamic and adaptable. It's on the move.

## 4. Compassion

Compassion is empathy in action. You feel your wife's pain and then do something about it. Whether the source of her hurt is her past, or some social drama, or you (!), you hear her out. Listen patiently and then act. Even if she's got it wrong you must avoid correcting here. This is how she *feels*. This is where mercy kicks in – mercy doesn't judge, it heals. You certainly are not your wife's doctor, psychologist, or messiah, but an affectionate listening ear will do wonders.

When living in Jerusalem years ago I had a good friend who was head of the Faculty of Psychiatry at the Hebrew University on Mount Scopus. Needless to say, he was a brilliant psychiatrist. One day during a break in our weekly squash game I asked him what were the essential components of effective psychiatry.

"There are three," he answered. "First is 95% listening. Second is 2-1/2% analyzing. Third is 2-1/2 % prescribing medication."

I was shocked. "You mean that if I am an effective listener I can help people almost as much as you do?" "Yep. You can." Wow! (Let it not be said of you, "He never listens"). Once you've really heard her you'll have a good idea of what course of action you should take. Compassion and communication go hand in hand.

### 5. Generosity

This is a no-brainer. Give more and more, not less and less. Let your giving of yourself be unqualified. If you're going to err, err on the side of abundance. Don't only give her your heart, but let your heart speak. She wants to know your innermost thoughts and feelings. So give, again and again. She'll respond in kind.

### 6. Flexibility

Rigidity in marriage guarantees fractures. You've got to be pliable, ready and able to bend without breaking. Friends are flexible. No friend every says, "My way or the highway!". If there's no room for compromise there's no room for love.

An immature person sees compromise as defeat. They don't want to settle, they want to win. Their intransigence often sees them bullying, forcing their way, intimidating with verbal abuse. Once they've got their way they're suddenly all sweetness and light, until the next time that is. They fear loss of control.

If one or both (!) of you tend to high control, tension will be a constant in your home. Conflict will be reminiscent of childhood wrangling, "Mine! No, mine! Give it back! It's mine! No, it's not!" The tug of war will wear you out. Little wonder you'll want separate vacations. Compromise, on the other hand, may see you walking that secluded beach together.

But remember that compromise is not compliance. Compliance yields, whereas compromise negotiates. If you're "giving in" just to keep the peace you may end up as a co-dependent, an enabler of your spouse's self-absorption. Walk that beach together, but let it be a destination that you agreed upon mutually. Let there be two adults on that long walk in the ocean breeze.

> *Let there be two adults on that long walk in the ocean breeze.*

## 7. Perseverance

I'm not referring to obstinacy, which is stubbornness in the face of and in spite of the facts ("Don't confuse me with facts"), and is essentially a negative trait. Rather, perseverance stays the course because it sees the end goal. It doesn't put its foot down, it puts its foot out. Perseverance is a journey. Your journey with your wife is day to day, year to year, horizon to horizon. Some days are dark, some years difficult, but the adventure continues. You're going somewhere and the joy truly is the journey. You keep at it.

These are some of the many colors of love. I call them "The Friendship Spectrum", a nexus of brilliance to light your way. And, as is always the case when light shines on us, we cast a shadow. Hidden in shadow, our flaws, weaknesses, and shortcomings may give us pause, but as we change our position the shadows flee. Committed love will empower us to make those changes. Over time we will thrive. As health and strength allow, one day you'll look back with sincere joy. You have loved that woman for all of her married life! Well done.

## SEVEN

# Our Love Story

You may have thought more than once while reading this book "So it's fine for him to say, but what would his wife say?" Well, you're going to hear from her. But before her thoughts (and the last word!) let me give you my overview of our love story.

I was standing with a group of other teenaged boys in the foyer of our church in Sudbury, Ontario, Canada. I was 15 years old. One of the boys and my 14-year-old brother had just returned from a visit to Southern Ontario where they had attended a church service the previous Sunday. They were going on and on about the pastor's daughter. She was gorgeous, all the guys in the church wanted to date her, all the mothers loved her, she was very outgoing, so popular, totally awesome… and they ran out of superlatives. I'm listening to this, my mind whirling with the mental image of this too-good-for-words girl and I blurt out, "You know what guys? I'm gonna marry her!" There were the predictable groans, gagging, and put downs – the consensus being that I was out of my mind. And maybe I was. Call it ego, extrasensory perception, or some sort of premonition, but I was convinced that I would one day marry this female wonder. Two years later I saw her for the first time.

My father had taken the pastorate of a church in southern Ontario. I was now 17 years of age. A few months into this new city, school, and church I had begun to casually date my boss's daughter (I worked part-time at his grocery store). One day she suggested we join the youth group of a church in a neighboring city on a bus trip to the graduating ceremony of a regional seminary in Toronto. Sure. Why not? I wasn't interested in the event but the bus trip with all those other kids would be fun. After the ceremonies at Massey Hall we all piled into the bus for the trip home. It was about 10pm as we sat in the dimness of the dome light at the entry door by the driver. When just about everyone had climbed in there was a bit of a flurry as a blonde head entered beneath that solitary light. I'll never forget the sight of her face as she smiled broadly and confidently said "Hi everyone!" The bus erupted with "Hey! Kathy! It's Kathy!" They all knew her except me. Her father had been their pastor for a few years, in fact she had been born in their city. She "worked the room" walking slowly down the aisle greeting everyone personally. When she came to where my date (I'll call her "Amy") and I were sitting she reached past me and high-fived her. As she moved on I turned to Amy and said, "Who's she?" With a bit of a dismissive tone, she put her arm in mine and answered, "Oh. That's Kathy Kerr." Kathy Kerr?! That's Kathy Kerr? That's the girl I'm going to marry! My heart leaped. This internal revelation changed my life. From that moment until now, all these decades later, I have been besotted with her. She is the love of my life.

I continued dating Amy throughout that winter. As summer approached she invited me to join her and her family at their cottage for a week in July. The cottage was located on the shore of Lake Ontario at a church camp called "Lakeshore Camp". That July week was "Youth Camp". There would be lots of new kids to meet and lots of fun. I asked her dad for that week off and he quickly complied. In fact, he said he'd take that week off too, and even drive me there. Awesome! I could hardly wait.

We arrived at the campgrounds late on a Saturday night. As we drove in he gave me a bit of advice – "Remember Jim, even though meeting several hundreds of kids seems intimidating, no one will meet anyone unless you take the initiative." As it turned out this bit of wisdom had a huge impact. We drove the long laneway to the cottage. On the way we suddenly saw a bunch of teenagers walking in the darkness. My boss said, "Maybe she's in this group," referring to his daughter. He stopped the car and as I got out I saw her there in the car's headlights, quickly withdrawing her hand from that of a boy I'd never met. The meeting was muted. There was stony silence as I joined her and others on the walk to a bonfire by the lake. When we got to the blaze she left me. There I was, alone with a bunch of strangers. That's when my boss's wise words kicked in.

I turned to the kids standing beside me in the firelight, offered my hand, and said, "Hi. I'm Jim Cantelon. Who are you?" Within a few minutes I'd already met several new teens. Then, looking across the fire to the strangers on the other side I saw her.

She was standing with her back turned, being accused by a guy holding the broken antenna of a walkie-talkie. I heard him say, "You broke it!" And her reply, "I think I sat on it by mistake." She sounded embarrassed. Suddenly I saw her in profile and my chest nearly burst. It was Kathy Kerr! The girl I was going to marry! Without thinking I immediately walked around the fire, went up to the guy and said, "I broke it!" (he knew I hadn't) and turned to Kathy and said, "Hi! I'm Jim Cantelon. Who are you?" And the rest, as they say, is history.

That night on the walk back to her cottage Amy broke up with me (much to her parents' displeasure). "What! You invite Jim here for a week and you do this to him?" I was told later that it was not a a happy scene. When she showed up late for a youth meeting the next night I could see she had been crying. I felt sorry for her. I went up to her and said, "Look. Your Mom said I could take her car whenever I wanted. You get a few friends together while I go and get it. I'll drive us to the Dairy Queen for a milkshake." When I returned she had two boys and two girls waiting. We piled into the car and were off, my heart thumping, because one of the two girls was Kathy!

As we stood around at the DQ we found ourselves in couples: Amy and the "handholder" (!), Ken and Heidi (who eventually married), and, to my everlasting joy, Kathy and me. I couldn't believe it.

On the drive home Amy climbed into the back seat (to join Mr. Handholder) and Kathy climbed into the front. She leaned over to me, wrinkled her nose, and said, "Hi Jim!" I was smitten. I did, however, keep my eyes on the road.

After a few more days of youth camp we parted ways – both of us to our separate cities where our fathers were pastors. I saw her again for a couple of days in October, then she and her family left for Argentina where her father took up the presidency of a theological college in Buenos Aires. They returned two years later and we connected on weekends for a couple of months. I left for college in Saskatchewan shortly thereafter while she attended Teacher's College in Ottawa. As you can see we hardly saw each other over the course of five years. Our together time amounted to about three weeks total. So, how did we do it? Letters. Lots of letters. Hundreds of them. Years later, after moving homes a few times with boxes of these missives, I decided to build a bonfire and commit them to the flames. It takes hours to completely burn a few thousand pages tightly folded together. After a long time, letters turning to ashes, I had a sudden tinge of regret. I leaned into the fire and removed a corner of a page just as it was about to disappear. In my handwriting I read, "I love you." And I did. And I do...

The great thing about love is that it grows. It's a living adventure built on faithfulness, time, compromise, children, surprises (some good, some bad), humor, career, memories, "the slings and arrows of outrageous fortune" (thank you Shakespeare), and on and on. It's a flowing stream, not a stagnant pond. It nourishes the soul.

> *The great thing about love is that it grows. It's a flowing stream, not a stagnant pond. It nourishes the soul.*

It has been 57 years since Kathy and I met, 52 since we married. Our fathers officiated at our wedding. My dad took the first part so that her dad could walk her down the aisle. I'll never forget the look on his face as he ushered her in, a vision of beauty on his arm. He looked like he was in pain. Or was it the holiness of the moment? Or, as someone put it indelicately (that someone, perhaps, a father), did he feel like he was about to hand a Stradivarius over to a gorilla? Nevertheless, he delivered her to me and then performed the vows. The glorious girl beside me took my breath away. I covenanted to love her for life, as did she to me. That promise has endured, as solid a foundation as the Rock of Gibraltar.

## Kathy's Thoughts or "The Last Word"

So I'm weighing in...

Jim left off at the wedding. And a lovely wedding it was! "Un mariage en rose," said the French-Canadian dressmaker. Beautiful summer's day, rings and vows, flowers and confetti, surrounded by love and support. We were pretty young but we didn't know it at the time. Same values, similar ideals, we embraced life! I was enthralled with this handsome young guy that had popped into my life at a summer camp. He was enthusiastic about everything. Including me! We were ready to embark on life's great adventure, together.

And so it began.

We started life together in a cool apartment in mid-town Montreal, two young kids learning the ins and outs of new jobs, bonding, discovering each other – the sensual delights, the likes and dislikes... the realities: He snores! She sniffs!, bonding, eating out at every amazing restaurant in the fascinating new city, bonding, facing life's inevitable curves and disappointments, bonding, growing up really, but together. I like to say it was a good thing Jim was the older firstborn and more mature because he married the youngest child of older parents who was less than mature. When I think of some of the issues that I created – mountains out of molehills, really. Poor Jim. He was patient. And kind. All those good things. And maturity kicked in, gradually but surely.

The newlyweds left the big city. Bought their first home. Had their first baby. Expanded their life in so many new directions. "If a door opens, walk through it!" was our guiding star. And the doors kept opening. Called to rescue a broken church. Invited to plant an international church – on the other side of the world. Hired to produce daily television. Incorporating a charitable organization in response to the AIDS pandemic. Three children and twelve grandchildren later, fifteen moves, teaching, television work, relief & development, international travel, did I mention fifteen moves?, and suddenly in the blink of an eye, it's been fifty years adventuring through life together!

> *Fifty years of marriage is no small thing.*

Fifty years of marriage is no small thing. To mark the occasion we'd planned a big celebration at a country inn along the shores of the Credit River – The Fam', the wedding party, closest friends. Perfect. But then the COVID pandemic reared its ugly head and put an end to that plan. Celebration is still on hold. The marriage, however, is still intact.

The younger set is amazed. "Do you mind if I ask you how you did it?", asks the lovely young manager at 'El Paradiso' where we're enjoying our 51st. "When I'm out with my girl friends I have to ask them to stop trashing their husbands. Favorite topic." So I stop and think. How DID we do it?

Well we didn't "trash" each other, for one.

I hate hearing "well you have to *work* at it!" Anything that's too much work gets old pretty quick. Of course there are moments in a marriage relationship when some work is required, not unlike any relationship, but the overall experience should be happiness and joy. It's your closest friendship, after all. So I wouldn't put "work at it" at the top of my list. I think it would have to be LOVE as number one. If you love someone you care for them like you care for yourself. Or as one young husband put it, "YOU first!"

Many wedding ceremonies quote these ancient words from the Bible:

> *Love is patient, love is kind, never jealous or*
> *envious, never boastful or proud, never*
> *haughty or selfish or rude.*
> *Love does not demand its own way.*
> *It is not irritable or touchy. It does not hold grudges*
> *and will hardly even notice when others do it*
> *wrong.*

I call it the Love Standard. When impatience, unkindness, selfishness, irritation break into the relationship these words are like an anchor yanking me/us back to my/our first love position. Like a hard drive reboot.

Realtors like to say that the three most important things in selling homes are location, location and location. I'd say the three most important things in a marriage, after the love foundation, are commitment, commitment, and commitment. When I was embarking on marriage as a young 21-year-old, I had absolutely no thought of a divorce option. I remember my Mom saying, as we did the final tweak on the wedding guest list, "Kathy-dear, if you have any troubles don't come home to Daddy and me, cause we won't be home. We're going to Argentina for the next year-and-a-half. You and Jim have to work things out." You're IN this. You're committed. If there are troubles you don't run for the exit. You run to each other's arms.

Interesting, isn't it, how we are so committed to our children, through thick and thin, through hell and high water,

> *Commitment to someone means you value that someone. Like a dearly loved child. But more so.*

no matter what kind of rotten behavior they're exhibiting, the commitment, and underlying love, seem to overcome all else. Why are we this way with our kids and not with each other? I wonder if it's because we've let the bond with each other grow weak and frayed. Like the drift of a boat. Left untended it begins to gradually float away, meandering downstream, farther and farther, until it begins to sink and you've lost it. And you hardly noticed. Commitment to someone means you value that someone. Like a dearly loved child. But more so.

Then there are the other three 'most' important marriage must haves: communication, communication and communication. Jim and I are both communicators. I'm the extrovert, he the introvert, but talkers both! So many ways to communicate, verbal, nonverbal, written, listening, visual. But you have to be in communication. I don't like hearing "we lead very independent lives" from married friends. Like ships passing in the night. That usually means the drift has begun. Don't let it happen. You're building a beautiful life together.

I love what one young husband said about marriage:

> *"It's pretty simple I think.*
> *Find out what your wife wants and needs...*
>   *and give it to her!*
> *Then find out what she really doesn't like about you...*

> *and stop doing it!*
> *She will do the same for you...*
> *and you'll be happy."*

Pretty simple really.

www.ingramcontent.com/pod-product-compliance
Lightning Source LLC
LaVergne TN
LVHW051608070426
835507LV00021B/2832